CW01346204

Somewhere Over the Rainbow

An autobiography of the life, love and loss of a 'Northchurch' girl

by
Linda Pottinger

authorHOUSE®

AuthorHouse™ UK Ltd.
500 Avebury Boulevard
Central Milton Keynes, MK9 2BE
www.authorhouse.co.uk
Phone: 08001974150

This book is a work of non-fiction. Unless otherwise noted, the author and the publisher make no explicit guarantees as to the accuracy of the information contained in this book and in some cases, names of people and places have been altered to protect their privacy.

© 2007 Linda Pottinger. All rights reserved.

No part of this book may be reproduced, stored in a retrieval system, or transmitted by any means without the written permission of the author.

First published by AuthorHouse 12/6/2007

ISBN: 978-1-4343-4299-7 (sc)

Printed in the United States of America
Bloomington, Indiana

This book is printed on acid-free paper.

Be honest and know truth,
Be strong and have faith,
Be still and feel peace,
Open your heart and find love

I dedicate this book to my darling husband, Richard (Dick) Pottinger who gave a purpose and richness to all things in my life.

Dick provided me with the inspiration to pursue my dreams, no matter how big or small and in my promise to never stop writing I fulfil his wishes in this, my autobiography. While our life together was tragically cut short, our love 'will always be' – no one can take that away. I move forward with profound thanks for the indelible footprints he has left in this world and for the strength and healing he has bestowed upon me.

Linda Pottinger.

Linda Pottinger has had a number of articles published in local magazines, such as Hertfordshire Countryside, Buckinghamshire Countryside and Cambridgeshire Pride, as well as Trades Journals and Hobbyist magazines. 'Somewhere Over the Rainbow' is her first book.

CONTENTS

Dedication v

Author Information vi

Chapter 1   Little Red Wellies 1

Chapter 2   Winky Pops 15

Chapter 3. The Puppy Love Era 26

Chapter 4   From Baby Blue… 44

Chapter 5   …To Chequered Band 57

Chapter 6   The Green, Green Grass of Home 74

Chapter 7   Chasing Rainbows 80

Chapter 8   He Ain't Heavy 88

Chapter 9   That Was The week That Was 100

Chapter 10 The Pot of Gold 108

Chapter 11 Rainbow's End 146

Chapter 12 Somewhere Over the Rainbow 169

CHAPTER 1

LITTLE RED WELLIES

You took me here, you took me there -
Together we went everywhere;
Wreaking havoc, my guiding star -
Oh yes, dear 'wellies we went far!

Like a child clinging to its comfort blanket, I was firmly glued to my little red wellies. How I loved them – we really went places, from dawn 'til dusk – I would have worn them in bed if I could. So fondly do I regard them, I refer to this early period of my life as the 'little red welly years'- for together we wreaked havoc and had fun.

I must have got through several pairs before they were finally consigned to the scrapheap. I was mortified at their demise; but, quite typically, it was all my own fault. I simply couldn't resist walking into the hot embers of a good old blizzy – otherwise known as a bonfire. We'd danced through snow, kicked leaves, been buried in mud and tripped the light fantastic until I melted them on that fateful day.

I arrived in the world at home in Berkhamsted – a sunny morning, 5th October 1961 – with a mop of dark hair. My brother Martin, a flaxen haired toddler, had already been around for two and a half years.

At six months old we moved in with my dad's parents at the other end of town, in Dell Road, Northchurch, and Grandma and Grandpy Delderfield became a very focal part of my life – especially Gramps, who I simply adored.

Mum, dad, Martin and I were crammed into one bedroom at the bungalow – named 'Gaza' after Grandpy's wartime postings. What impact it had on mum and dad's personal life I can only imagine – three is a crowd, let alone four.

The bungalow was bone-chilling cold – you wouldn't tarry too long in the basic bathroom or toilet. Oh, how I hated the toilet paper – 'Izal' – hard, scratchy and absorbed next to nothing. We had a posh front room that was only ever inhabited at Christmas. I guess it was the coldest room in the house as it faced north. Inside was a lovely sideboard with artefacts on top, including a wooden biscuit barrel, with silver shield on the side. I remember the barrel, particularly, as much later this was the only object my dad chose to be left to him on Grandpy's death – he never actually got it and so I can only assume it fell into the hands of other family members in the end.

The attic was used as a store for the apples from the small orchard in the back garden – they were spread out neatly in rows on newspaper. Getting to them was precarious on a rickety ladder. Despite my enquiring mind and the lovely views over the common it wasn't an area I liked – it was spooky, far too many cobwebs to negotiate – a poke around was fun, but not worth risking an encounter with a hairy spider.

The heart of the bungalow was the kitchen – our real living room. It was dominated by a large farmhouse table and Grandpy's rocking chair – no one else sat in it, and Grandma had an armchair by the fire. There was a small wooden footstool that, when I wasn't perched on it, was used by Grandpy's weary legs.

In a corner next to the cooker stood a large copper where Grandma spent ages with big wooden-handled tongs, prodding and poking the washing. I enjoyed watching her use the mangle best – even better if I got a go at turning the handle. Literally everything went in that copper – but most of all it reminds mum of 'Grandma's knickers'. When they were past decent, Grandma would boil them in the copper then cut out the best bits. These were then used as the cloth wrap to go round the beef dumpling. The image today still renders mum hysterical and she is eternally grateful the knickers and a joint of boiling bacon didn't occupy the copper at the same time! The copper was also the main feature of bath-night, when, after boiling, the water had to be hand-carried into the bathroom to fill the bath. Mum often gave up and went to her parents to take a bath. Martin and I sat in an old tin bath in front of the kitchen fire. I still have vague recollections of this – it seems infinitely preferable to the chill of the bathroom.

On the cooker – or rather, hanging on a wire above, was the frying pan – with the solidified dripping in it from its last outing! Just one look was enough to clog the arteries – but, if nothing else, it kept the chill off the bones. In the opposite corner a small sideboard housed Grandpy's huge pickling jar and his home-produced pickled onions. They lasted ages and were fantastic – I've yet to taste one better.

Another sideboard was decked with plates, jugs and a lovely Swiss-looking clock with a pretty blue and white willow-type pattern dial. When Grandpy died years later, this was left to my dad – but it never worked since. The television moved about a few times but I recall it being in the corner near the copper.

Undoubtedly the 'piece de resistance' was the coal fire – we'd all cling to its warmth, although the big fireguard was essential to prevent me from trying to prod the coals. I was that sort of child – a pest, inquisitive and foolhardy. Winter was the only time we ever had toast or crumpets – sitting round with the toasting fork on the embers and buttered toast never, ever, tasted *so good*.

One Sunday we had such excitement – the chimney caught fire! Dad and Grandpy tried to put it out from indoors to no avail. Dad then put a ladder against the roof and managed to get it out by pouring water down the chimney stack. Oh, what joy, what fun! We caused quite a stir along the back road, and everyone came to watch. The heat caused a great crack in the chimney breast. The kitchen looked like a bomb site, with soot and water all over the place, but who cared – certainly not me – especially as I got out of going to Sunday school!

We had a big front garden with vegetables grown in abundance – in fact I don't recall us ever buying any – maybe just a few sacks of potatoes. I picked fresh mint for many years to come.

The back garden was smaller, with an orchard to one side, backed by a hen run – or hen'us (hen house) as it was known. Grandma kept chickens, although the foxes were a nuisance, and I remember dad and Grandpy going off up the road after them with their shotguns. I especially recall returning with mum from a Sunday school trip to Littlehampton – all the chickens had been destroyed by the fox. Is it my imagination – or did I really see headless chickens still running about the hen'us?

There was a large potting shed (draped with thick stringy cobwebs), a smaller shed, two large greenhouses and large cold frame. It was a bit tricky walking between and around the greenhouses, for scrap timber, glass and junk stacked precariously against things – guess there was the 'never throw anything away – you never know when it might come in useful' ethic. The whole plot only occupied a quarter of an acre but not an inch was wasted. Food was never taken for granted – and self-sufficiency was important to help stretch the money each week.

I loved collecting the eggs – marvelling that some were white, some brown, and many were still warm. I'm sure the essence of what we had at home gave dad his yearning to be a farmer. Grandpy wouldn't sanction it as there was no money in it then, so he became a painter and decorator instead. He would have been a good farmer – he loved the countryside and rejoiced to see the land being worked – how he hated seeing fields left fallow. I, too, would have been in my element. Oh, just how much further my adventurous red wellies would have travelled – what extra mischief would have been on offer?

Visitors to the house included gypsies selling heather. Grandma always bought a sprig – believing it bad luck to turn them away. I was plain curious about them. We also had unannounced visits by our relations from Watford – invariably rolling up at dinner or tea-time – Walt, Rene and seven more children to feed – no mean feat. Another excitement for me was when dad got knocked off his bicycle by the baker's van. He was confined to bed and we called the doctor out. He had a nasty gash on his leg and the wheel on his bicycle was all smashed up. I found it all fascinating. It happened again later – this time he was grounded by the milkman. I have to say dad wasn't much better in a car but at least he didn't get hurt.

`The area we lived in was known as 'Pikey's Island'. Many of the properties were owned by a Mr Pike who rented them out, although Grandpy proudly owned his own bungalow – one of the very few homeowners in the area at that time. Mr Pike wanted to sell the house next door - number three, so dad bought it – a big, cold, damp semi-detached property. The tenants, Mr and Mrs Walls, rented it on until they both died. When I reached the ripe old age of four years we moved in, giving peace and freedom back to my grandparents - but I still spent much time at the bungalow. Often I'd come home from school and go to sit with Grandma. She was diabetic, with failing eyesight, so when I was starting to read well, I would regale her with news from the weekly Gazette.

Grandma, though I never heard it, could really shout when the need arose. Dad recalled being 'bellowed' home from the rec' (recreation ground) on many an occasion. Bear in mind this area now has four rows of houses between 'Gaza' and the former A41 main road and stretches some four-six hundred yards away. I guess in those days there was far less traffic noise and not such a density of houses blocking the way – nevertheless, a good town crier she would have made!

One Christmas Grandma gave mum a pretty Dutch apron – lovely, except mum had bought it for her the previous year. Mum never let on and still chuckles about it now.

F.A. Cup Final day was always spent at the bungalow. Dad had been a great local player in his day – a very fast runner (no one ever beat him in the regular village mile race) and a prolific goal-scorer. I'd take my dolls with me, yet watch the game. My poor dolls – how they suffered! They were never pretty for long as I often decided to change their hairstyles – which actually meant I simply cut their hair with scissors. Unfortunately they hadn't yet invented dolls with hair that grew back – hence mine always looked a state.

It wasn't just the dolls that fell prey to the scissors – one day my wellies and I disappeared into the front garden away from view – I decided it was time my own hair needed cutting and promptly took clumps out from over my forehead. Mum had apoplexy, rushed me to the hairdressers and I sported a very short style for a few weeks to come! Mum got her own back as she always gave me a centre parting, grips and slides – thanks mum – have you any idea how long it took me to get rid of that parting?!

I'm not sure I was happy being a girl. I preferred the rough and tumble tomboy life – going headfirst over the neighbour's fence to retrieve a ball, or to scrump apples. Of course, it was always me that got caught.

When I had just turned ten years old, Grandma had a stroke. Grandpy thumped on our door early one morning, fit to wake the dead. Dad rushed to mum's parents opposite to phone the doctor. She was admitted to hospital, and just when she seemed to be improving, she passed away. I didn't understand what death was all about, but it hurt to see Grandpy so upset.

Mum's parents were Nanny and Grandpy Sear. Nanny wouldn't let us call her Grandma. We often went for Sunday tea, and Grandpy would have Grandstand on the television. A chiming clock heralded each new hour in its homely tone. We had tea up at the table, beautifully laid out. There were lovely cakes and a cake-stand I coveted. Nanny wore her Sunday best, and I would mind my Ps and Qs.

On the wall above the television was an oil picture – a portrait of my mother, Barbara Mary, aged fourteen years, painted by Mrs Winifred Forster, a lady for whom Nanny cleaned. Mum would go to her house after her weekly cookery class, she would be given her tea and then had to sit for her to do the painting. It really is a rather good portrait – very identifiable as mum at that age.

Mum had two younger siblings - her brother Brian who now lives in Wales, and the youngest child Kath. Aged nine years old mum spent a lot of her time looking after her brother and sister, while her parents were working. You grew up early in those days.

Grandpy Sear had a rasping wheezy chest. He was asthmatic and used an inhaler a lot. He wasn't in good health and died not long after Grandma Delderfield. Mum's childhood was not a happy one – with great unrest and many an argument in the home, so much so that when mum married dad, she vowed there would be no arguments in front of us children – and there never were. Keeping her own childhood to herself she just made sure that Martin and I had a wonderful one – a precious gift for which I thank her dearly.

Nanny had favourites – suffice to say it wasn't us. My Auntie Kath, Uncle Rod and Cousins Sharon and Carol moved to the bungalow next to Nanny and Grandpy Sear when I was still a young child, and the door to me with Nanny seemed forevermore closed. Nanny had never accepted my dad so I was in prestigious company.

I tried *so* hard as a child to please Nanny but it was futile and in the end I gave up trying – with a deep hurt that never left me. Even the sentimental poems I used to write inside birthday cards had little effect – I was quite a bard in those days. When she died much later on, my tears were for mum's pain and for missing out on the chance of a loving relationship with Nanny.

Mum remembers well during World War Two, when they had two different families of refugees stay with them from London. The first was a large Jewish family – they took over the whole of the living room as nowhere else would have been big enough for them. After they had gone, there was a mother and daughter who stayed awhile.

Mum and dad both talked of wartime - watching dogfights overhead and the day the doodlebug landed on Northchurch

Common. It must have been terrifying, although for children maybe tinged with some excitement too.

Then there was Great Grandma Sear – who, when I was still an infant, was living with Nanny and Grandpy. She occupied the back bedroom and was predominantly bed-bound. She had a Zimmer frame to move about with and she used to plait her hair so neatly on top of her head – I always thought it made her look like a German fraulein. The most memorable thing about Great Grandma, however, was her glass eye. Many a time we would be visiting at her bedside and this glass eye would be observing me from the bedside cabinet – it was a very scary experience for a young girl. Even worse than being 'eyeballed' was the fact that great Grandma had one empty eye socket at such times – now that was *even scarier*. I used to pray with every visit that the eye would be in its rightful place!

I don't much recall Great Grandpy Sear, save a fleeting memory of going to their house in Castle Street, Berkhamsted with mum. I don't think we went in, just stood at the door – Great Grandpy answered – a large framed man who filled the doorway.

My schooling began at Northchurch, St Mary's Church of England Primary School (as it had for my parents, and Grandma and Grandpy Delderfield before me). In their day it had been one small building only, with the Working Men's Club and the Church Room occupying part of the land where the new section of the school was added in the early 1960s. For both mum and dad this was their only seat of formal education - both left at fourteen years of age to begin their working lives.

I loved school – I was a slow starter, never having been to nursery school, but picked up good speed by the age of ten and was proud as punch when I was awarded the School Prize in 1972 – in the shape of a leather bound Book of Common Prayer.

I remember well, the star charts, where you were given tasks to do – such as tying a shoelace, or bow and were rewarded with your star once accomplished. We had very regular spelling tests and times tables to learn. We would chant them out as a class or you could be picked out individually to recite a table. I loved spellings, but also enjoyed learning tables – they were the most valuable thing – once learned they stay with you for life.

The Headmaster was Fred Phillips, a strict disciplinarian, who went bright red in the face when angry – it wasn't a good idea to cross his path! He was also a lay-preacher at St Mary's Church next door. Mr Phillips still used the cane or slipper in those days – unlike Miss Pickles, who needed neither to inflict her pain – I can still hear the resounding slap on many a child's leg and the red hand-shaped mark that took ages to fade.

Thankfully I did not take after my father, who was neither the brightest nor best behaved schoolboy of his time. Mum recalls in particular, a teacher called Miss Margrave, who used to be played up terribly by the boys – she would chase them around the classroom - dad amongst them. The headmaster in her day, Gaffer Gibbs would constantly tap a cane against his leg - poised ready for action upon any miscreant.

Mr Phillips held my respect always, and I appreciated the values he set which I took with me for later in life. He worked us hard and played us hard. A particular highlight was always May Day, with our maypole dancing – so colourful, and the only time I could ever be accused of being remotely graceful. I also loved Sports Day on the adjacent field, where my first best friend, the extremely pretty, Lynda Haysman was always fastest in our class.

Lynda and I sat together – collectively known as the 'two Lindas' (or should it be Lynda's?) I loved tea at her house – we always had oven-baked sausages, beans and mash – truly scrumptious. There were lovely 'sing-alongs' in the house, with Lynda's dad playing guitar - a wonderful family atmosphere. Her younger brother and sister, Terry and Tina, were twins. Terry was known as Bobby, avoiding confusion with his dad, Terry senior. Bobby was a really talented scallywag, a daredevil with a smile to illuminate any room.

One morning we watched a pair of legs coming down New Road, Northchurch – it was Bobby, walking to school on his hands. Another day he fainted while having a contest with another boy to see who could hold their breath the longest – guess he won!

Dear Bobby tragically died aged nine years old. He dangled wire onto the overhead power lines of the railway near the entrance to Northchurch tunnel. In a flash of light he was thrown headlong to the tracks where he fractured his skull. The combination of the massive electric shock and damaged skull, proved too much even for Bobby to endure. Bobby was born to be 'someone' in adulthood, but as it happened, he remains a wonderfully gifted child, indelibly etched in the memories of those who knew him. To this day I have never been able to walk along the adjacent Grand Union Canal with the tunnel entrance in sight, without thinking of Bobby.

Other friends included Liz May, whose mother was into amateur dramatics – I particularly remember a birthday party at her house, which was attended by a very young Sarah Brightman – of course no-one could have imagined how famous she was to become at that time. There was also Lynne Jarvis, who had a wonderful kidney-shaped dressing table that I would simply have died for. She also had a lovely border collie dog called 'Smokey'. Lynne, Liz and I used to play elastic skipping, amongst other games – I remember being picked on as I was both the youngest and smallest.

I received a never-ending stream of suitcases containing Lynne's cast-off clothes throughout my childhood as mum and dad couldn't afford brand new very often. I remember with acute embarrassment, an episode of wearing an emerald green dress – courtesy of Lynne. It was during my days in the Junior Church choir. I was reading the lesson in St Mary's Church, which was quite a regular occurrence as my voice carried well without the need for microphones that most churches employ today. With Lynne, being both bigger framed and more advanced in 'shapely development', so to speak, I needed to put a bit of padding in my first brassiere to fit this dress properly.

How did I manage to stand in church reading a lesson with half a ton of Kleenex at my underdeveloped bosoms? I feel sure now that everyone must have noticed. There must have been some sniggering in the choir stalls if nothing else – but if so, credit where it's due, no-one was cruel enough to point it out to me.

Then there was Janet Wheatley. I was amazed that she had the same birthday as me – a fascinating coincidence for an infant. Over the years we played many a skipping game in her back garden – halcyon days of 'I'm a little bumper car'. Oh yes, I remember one occasion when the 'bumper' car became reality. Janet collided with a tin of paint her dad had just opened –its contents gushing out over the patio. Being equally culpable, after poor Janet had a slap on the legs I felt I needed to make a sharp exit that day – for once, without taunting her elder brother, Stephen by calling him 'Weetabix'.

I later had the pleasure of working alongside Steve in the police force and we enjoyed some merciless rib-pulling and banter that comes only from sharing a childhood.

My closest, long-standing best friend was Karen Spencer. We became friends in our last year at Northchurch primary school, probably through our brothers, Martin and Ian, being best buddies. Karen was in many ways the opposite of me. She was very sweet and 'girlie' and good at all things domesticated – she had a beautiful hand with a needle, and became a good cook. I, on the other hand, was still this mad tomboy, with a shout to match Grandma Delderfield's and trying to keep up and compete with my brother as a little hooligan. I guess it was a case of opposites attracting, as we got on so well. Although we went to different middle schools (they were an innovation in Berkhamsted) we shared much time together and were almost inseparable throughout the summer holidays. Our friendship is intrinsically linked to what I refer to as the 'Puppy Love' era and deal with later.

Many years later I became a governor at Northchurch School for a year or so. It was wonderful walking through the corridors again – except, of course, they appeared to have shrunk in length and height considerably. The area of clothes hooks and gym bags also seemed minuscule – naturally, aged five to nine years everything is in miniature except the physical dimensions of the building.

Aside from friends I was also duty bound to spend much time with my cousins Sharon and Carol. In latter school years I used to help Sharon with her maths homework. We would listen to music together, dance to Auntie Kath's Helen Shapiro records and eat my aunt's gorgeous home-cooked chips.

These days, of course, the little red wellies are but a thing of the past. Just thinking about them gives me delight – they symbolise fun, hardship and, most of all, the enduring love of my parents and grandparents.

Somewhere Over the Rainbow

Dad & his mum   Dad score the winner - again!

Gaza   Martin & me at Gaza

Grandma & Grandpy Delderfield

Linda Pottinger

Martin & me   With mum, dad & Martin   Nanny & Grandpy Sear

3 Dell Road

Kath, Nanny & mum   Me aged 11yrs

CHAPTER 2

WINKY POPS

"That'll stick to your ribs" I hear you say
Of mothers special stew,
And you always called me 'Winky Pops'-
The grandpy that I knew.

I am no different to many people who enjoyed growing up in a small nuclear family unit of four – my parents and brother kept me safe from harm, nurtured me through my school days into adolescence, and then allowed me to spread my wings into adulthood. Naturally they have been the most influential people in my life until later, much later; when they were joined by my husband.

There is, however, one other person, who coloured my childhood years, until his passing when I was fourteen years old – that being, my Grandpy Delderfield or 'Gramps'. His actual name was Ernest Frederick Delderfield – known as 'Fred' or 'Pimmer'. Where 'Pimmer' comes from is a mystery to all – it seems that the male Delderfields have always had this nickname, but no one knows either its origin or meaning.

Gramps was born on 8th May 1894, the son of James Delderfield, a gamekeeper and Mary Ann Bridges. He was the seventh of their nine children.

Gramps first worked as a milkman at the Castle Street dairy, Berkhamsted, then later as a gardener at Berkhamsted School - now The Collegiate School. He married Edith Kate Welling on 7th February 1920 at Northchurch St. Mary's and together they had five children, of which my father, Peter, was the fourth.

Dad was close only to his sister, my Auntie Joan, the firstborn child. Uncle Walt lived in Watford and blew in and out when he felt like it - with or without his wife, Auntie Rene and any number of their seven children. Uncle Ernie, married to Enid lived in Northchurch and although we did see a bit more of him and his family, I don't feel he and dad could ever be described as 'close'. We had always thought dad was the youngest child until Antony, a second cousin, once removed, researched our family tree.

Enter Donald - born in 1934, three years after dad. Donald was apparently born without muscles and died two months later. What astounds me is that no-one ever talked about him - certainly not my grandparents, nor Auntie Joan. Mum was unaware of his existence, and I imagine dad, at three years old would have little recall of a new infant.

An ill, damaged or deceased child, in those days appears to be an unspoken subject. I can only imagine this to be a trait passed down from generations who had endured the pain of losing so many children at birth or infancy.

Gramps called me 'Winky Pops' - a nickname that stuck like glue. To say I idolised him would be an understatement and to this day he remains a somewhat iconic figure to me

Having arrived in his home at six months old and not moving out until I was four - albeit only fifty feet or so to the house next door - I guess it gave us plenty of time for bonding. It makes me realise just how important influences at such a young age can be. For children who experience terrible abuse and cruelty, I can quite understand how difficult it must be to overcome these issues later in life. Thankfully for me, my memories are all good ones and I can cherish them forever.

Donning my red wellies, I would follow 'Gramps' everywhere - I was his perpetual shadow. I would sit on an upturned bucket while he worked in the large potting shed - peering cagily through the door on the lookout for spiders.

I was an ever-present fixture with him in his greenhouse as he tended lovingly to his carnations. Gramps had one greenhouse full of carnations and chrysanthemums - and was locally renowned for them – the carnations being his particular forte. The blooms were massive and their perfume exquisite. He had grown them for the Queen Mother's visit to Berkhamsted School in 1958. My favourite was a white carnation with a deep pink candy-stripe in it. If a flower head broke he would always give them to me, chucking me under the chin as he did so.

I remember frequently going with mum to deliver bunches of his carnations to people in the village – especially to Win Fenn in Seymour Road, and most frequently to Alice Bruton at Dropshort, the cottage opposite the 'rec.' which, historically, was a coach stop for weary travellers en route to London.

Gramps had a second greenhouse that housed mainly tomatoes and cucumbers. Trotting along behind, he would pluck off his first cherry tomatoes giving them to me to eat – they smelt and tasted divine.

Of course, not only did I follow Gramps like a sheep, I did so, chatting nineteen to the dozen as we went, not coming up for air, as he worked in one spot or other. If it was peace and quiet he was after, he was in the wrong company.

Gramps had a highly infectious laugh. As he chuckled, so his eyes creased in the corners, hence a fine set of crow's feet in older age. He had the most wonderful sparkle in his blue-grey eyes – they twinkled like the stars – but unlike Great Grandma Sear's, they didn't come out at night! He had what mum and I call the 'Delderfield' hands: as large as shovels, but bony, with noticeable veins. Certainly Gramps, dad and my brother's hands were identical with mine being a slightly smaller, more feminine version. Like my father, Gramps was not a man of sartorial elegance, although some photographs of him as a young man show him to be very debonair when suited and booted. Like many of his peers, he would wear a suit, or jacket and trousers at home, work and for going out – though – not necessarily the same one! He wore his shirtsleeves rolled up and always sported braces – keeping the look together – literally. Gramps' jacket would invariably be hanging on the doorknob of the greenhouse or shed while he worked. I can't recall ever seeing him in shoes (although I imagine he had some for best) – he always wore hefty boots. He often donned a flat cap when the weather was cold – you would find it hanging on a nail in the shed or greenhouse. He also wore waistcoats or knitted v-necked, short-sleeved tank tops.

Gramps, like my father, didn't wear a wristwatch, preferring a pocket fob watch on a chain. While working in the garden, another accessory he was rarely without, was a roll-up cigarette – mum would regularly get him his ounce of Old Holborn and blue papers. To this day I love the smell of Old Holborn which evokes his memory. He enjoyed the odd tot of whisky too – mainly as he got older and to keep colds at bay, but never to excess, as, like my dad he was no drinker.

If it seems, in my biased view, that Gramps was without fault – then of course that isn't so. Like everyone, no doubt he had many human failings. Personally, I can only remember one – his cooking! Being at the village primary school enabled me to come home midday for dinner. Many times when mum accompanied Grandma to the hospital for check-ups on her diabetes, I had to go to 'Gaza' for dinner 'à la Gramps'. Invariably that frying pan came into play with potatoes, sausages and eggs on the menu. The eggs always floated in grease with brown bits attached from the sausages. In those days I was a fussy eater and would only eat potatoes if fried anyway – but he never encouraged my appetite.

Food, naturally, is a matter of personal taste – how Gramps ever could eat tripe and onions was beyond me – likewise, bread and dripping. I know it was once common fare, but am sure I would rather have starved. He also liked cold broad beans – black-eyed, at that – which I am assured are ones past their best. Of course – nothing was wasted.

Mum recalls that they never used table salt - Grandma had blocks of cooking salt and would grind some off into a little bowl that would grace the dining table. Between the levels of fat and sodium I am astounded Gramps lived to be eighty-two years old.

Mum marvels at the fact that Grandma and Gramps always had a proper cooked breakfast, a midday main meal, afternoon biscuits or cake, a proper tea, followed by supper later in the evening. To look at Gramps slender frame you wouldn't have believed it possible. They treated food as 'manna from heaven.' Dad always remembered when having food was something of a luxury. Many a time Gramps would come home from work, find there was nothing for dinner (save vegetables, undoubtedly) and have to go out and shoot rabbits for the meal. Dad would often accompany him, and was eternally grateful that Gramps was such an excellent shot – apparently he didn't miss much!

My dad, strangely, was a very fussy eater – plain food only for him. He never liked mushrooms and would only eat onions of the pickled variety. The mere sight of spaghetti made him feel ill – a throwback from his army days when it regularly appeared at the serving hatch like a 'bowl of worms'- eek! I, for one, took ages to eat potatoes normally. First they had to be fried, and then I acquiesced to having them boiled or mashed, but only if served up with lashings of brown sauce! It wasn't until I went to Middle School – The Augustus Smith School, at the other end of Berkhamsted, and had to partake of school dinners, that I succumbed to plain potatoes. From then on I ate anything, even mushrooms and onions, which like dad, I hadn't previously liked.

Mum used to make wonderful bacon or beef dumplings and a stew to die for. Gramps, tickling me under the chin would say "That'll stick to your ribs, Winky Pops", with the old familiar chuckle. I guess much of our food was for energy and to stave off the cold, as well as being economical. The Sunday joint of lamb (or mutton), which was cheaper then, was always finished off cold on Monday with baked beans and mash. Beef was hitherto unheard of as it was way beyond our budget.

Even living next door, I would chat to Gramps over the fence as he was digging, or planting vegetables. I loved watching him with his dibber making holes for his seed potatoes or plants and took every opportunity to help out – another excuse to play in the mud and get plastered.

I watched in fascination as the robin redbreast hopped about near his feet as he toiled, turning soil and presenting the robin with easy worms to feed on. No sooner had Gramps stuck the fork in the ground and walked away from it, the robin would fly onto the handle. I love birds in the garden and a robin, apart from Christmas, always makes me think of Gramps. How strange that we make association in the smallest of ways. On a similar vein, a blackbird, for me is intrinsically linked to my dad. He loved his 'blackies' and they frequently nested in the hedge at the top of the garden. Since my dad's passing, the song of the blackbird makes him ever closer.

Ironically on my wedding day, in beautiful Castle Combe, Wiltshire, the first thing I saw in the morning was a blackbird. It sat on the roof of a building opposite, singing its heart out. It got the day off to a sublime start – dad was there with me!

Grandma and Gramps had been members of the local Darby and Joan club, although Gramps didn't venture far after Grandma died. I can recall him babysitting for us one Christmas, when mum and dad had gone to dad's works Christmas do. Martin and I shared a bedroom in those days. I missed mum and dad and was crying in my bed. I can still hear Gramps calling up to me "Are you all right Winky Pops?" and Martin – who must have thought me a right pain, kindly saying I was just missing mum and dad.

After losing Grandma, Gramps came round to us each day for dinner (we always ate our main meal at midday). I used to pester him for war stories – he always, I'm sure, told me the same things, but the answers elude me now. It wasn't until his mobility diminished that we would take his dinner round to him instead. I used to love that little errand – although I couldn't tarry long or else my own meal would be cold.

Gramps had a love of horse racing – or the 'gee gees' as he called them. He'd have a little flutter most weekends, like dad – and dad would take the bets to Johnson's bookies in town for him. They never bet much – a couple of quid here or there at best. It was the sport they enjoyed. They liked studying and discussing the form – though why they did is a mystery to me – it didn't seem to help them any. Gramps would go straight to the racing pages of his newspaper and put pencil marks all over it. He enjoyed television, especially for the racing and football – I'm sure he would have loved colour T.V, alas he only ever possessed a black and white one as far as I remember.

'Gee gees' also provided another valuable commodity for the garden – their manure. Dad was frequently sent down the road with a pail and shovel – to collect any droppings left by the horses pulling carts and deliverymen through the village. I was reminded of this recently, when in Bricket Wood I saw a notice pinned to a telegraph pole on the footpath. There are a few equestrian centres in the vicinity and the horses are exercised early in the mornings. A few spatterings of manure hit the footpaths and the author of the notice had beseeched "Would horse riders not leave their droppings on the footpath – it is most unpleasant". Ho hum...I guess the disgruntled person never thought to use it on the garden – how times have changed.

I can also visualise Grandpy's stack of newspapers – piled neatly to the left of the cooker – it was always useful for laying fruit out on, peeling spuds on, and for setting the coal fire. The stack in latter years exceeded the use to which it was put and grew mountainous!

Mum would regularly go round to clean for Gramps. She would clean around him as he sat at the table in his rocking chair, his 'baccy' on the table.

Gramps heart was broken when his eldest son Walter (Walt) and wife Irene (Rene) split up. As a staunch Baptist – albeit not a regular attendee at services, he felt the pain of their parting keenly, even changing his will as a result. Mum said he used to sit at the table crying about it. It hurts so much to think of my ever-smiling Gramps in tears – I would most certainly have cried with him.

At middle school we were doing a project on the war. Gramps to the rescue! To my delight Gramps gave me his

World War I brass box – which they were given at Christmas 1915. The greeting card from Princess Mary was still inside, together with the bullet pencil – this being a bullet which when pulled apart contained a small pencil.

He also gave me his war postcards – twenty in all, many of which had his written messages on the back, still legible today. Gramps let me keep them, and I am privileged to still have them. I recently transcribed the ones he had written and have taken copies of them all, to preserve their image in case their condition deteriorates. The tin used to sit on the mantelpiece in his bedroom and Grandma had proudly polished it until it gleamed – in hindsight this is a shame as she eroded much of the etched detail.

Gramps war medals are with my cousin, Robin, and I recently got to view them for the first time, together with the old Family Bible. He had been in different sections – he was a driver in the Hertfordshire Regiment (with a star shaped medal etched with his number 871); he was also a gunner in the Royal Field Artillery (a medal on a red, white & blue sash etched with his number 890666). He has George V medal 1914-1918 on an orange sash and a medal on a rainbow striped ribbon – the Great War for Civilisation 1914-1919 etched with his number 357252 – this was his number when he was a gunner in the Royal Garrison Artillery. How I wish I had paid more attention to the war stories I took from him. He did tell me he had a horse fall on him and crush his foot, but beyond that my memory is deplorably thin. One thing Gramps didn't tell me that I recall, was that he had an elder brother James who tragically lost his life, aged thirty-three years, at the Somme, in 1918. He is at rest at Puchevillers British Cemetery in France and I intend to get to the grave in the future to pay respects to a Great Uncle that I never got to meet. As luck would have it a client of mine took his own father on a Battlefields tour in France. They visited Puchevillers and he kindly photographed the gravestone, cemetery and site office book for me.

I was fourteen years old when Grandpy Delderfield died – in May 1976. Dad had gone round to check on him in the morning, as always. It must have been a Saturday as Martin and I were at home. Dad came back as white as a sheet. Just one glance at dad's face told me all I needed to know. Darling Gramps' heart had given out while getting into bed the night before. Oh, how I wish I could have been there, so he didn't move on alone. How I wish I could have told him how much I loved him – I experienced these same feelings all over again when my dad died in January 1997. The things left unsaid – how I curse myself. I beseech you – tell your loved ones just how much they mean to you while you can.

I was so upset that mum and dad said I didn't have to attend the funeral if I felt I couldn't cope with it. For that I was grateful, as a very naïve, immature fourteen year old, I wouldn't have held up any too good! As it was I was going to my friend, Karen's for the duration. I was upstairs in my bedroom when the hearse arrived. It simply ripped me apart seeing the coffin – I was right not to go to the funeral – I would have made it worse for everyone else. I ran to Karen's in floods of tears that seemed to last all day. I was heartbroken.

Although Nanny Sear berated me for not attending – telling me I owed it to my Grandad to go, I know mum and dad were wiser. I couldn't respect or adore Gramps more than I did then or do now. I was with him every second of the funeral and he, like my dad, remains firmly entrenched in my heart and mind for all eternity.

My interest in family history has deepened, greatly assisted by second cousin Antony's family trees. He has tracked back through five generations of the Delderfield family, as well as the Welling family. As you look back down the generations there is a wealth of sadness in the evidently high infant mortality rates. Gramps had a Great Uncle Richard whose wife Sarah appears to have died in childbirth along with their first born son Richard. He remarried and, determined to continue his lineage, the first born son of this marriage was also baptised Richard – only for him to die aged five years. Such tragedies are hard to fully appreciate today – and I cannot imagine anyone now calling two children by the same name.

Snippets of social history are gleaned from family trees. Gramps father, my Great Grandad - James, was a gamekeeper - and no doubt passed on his shooting skills to Gramps. There are labourers, agricultural labourers, mantle makers, straw plaiters and domestic servants across both family trees.

I was fascinated to find that Grandma Delderfield's Aunt Emma married a Samuel Delderfield - thus starting another local branch of Delderfield's. Six out of their nine children were boys therefore it is little wonder that 'Delderfield' is a well-known name in Northchurch.

I have recollections of visiting dad's Aunt Mary in Tyttenhanger Green, St Albans as a child - she always gave me coleus plants, with their brightly-coloured leaves, to take home and nurture. Then there was dad's Aunt Ethel who lived in Seymour Road - in a tiny terraced cottage. I don't have memories of visiting other of dad's older relatives - I guess most were dead or had left the area.

My love of writing has re-awakened the desire in me to know more. It is now in particular, I wonder just how much of our heritage is lost by not asking questions of our elders – by not taking time to listen, probe and enquire. I so wish Gramps was here today – as an adult I have so many questions unanswered, so much I thirst to know of his life and family – all too late of course. I have wonderful old photographs, which I cherish – and I will always be, Gramps little Winky Pops.

Somewhere Over the Rainbow

Gramps - army days    Suited & booted    At work at 'Gaza'

Carnation greenhouse    With brother James (left)    With father James

Gramps & Grandma marry 1920    James' grave    Gramps medals

CHAPTER 3

THE PUPPY LOVE ERA

*I have days of red mist and long for a cuddle -
When my stomach is achy and my brain's all a fuddle.*

*These days when I'm tetchy nothing seems right,
I'm so clumsy or ratty, tense and uptight.*

*For pre-menstrual tension is an unexplained curse
That hits many women, some better, some worse.*

*The emotions are fragile, do you laugh, do you cry ?
And you think you've gone mad without realising why.*

*When you bark and you bite at problems so small,
Where tempers are lost and tears quick to fall.*

*When logic and reason like high spirits are forsaken,
Until the storm breaks and you feel quite mistaken.*

*That you couldn't possibly, so irrational have been,
And feel so guilty for those who encountered your spleen.*

*My mother will remember my most miserable hours
Followed by days of saying sorry with flowers.*

*My sympathy is deep for those whose suffering is worse
For I understand the frustration that comes with the curse.*

As the title of this chapter will suggest – to anyone having a knowledge of seventies music and pop icons – this was my Osmond mania time. Donny Osmond was my absolute idol – not only was he *such a handsome dreamboat* – he was destined to marry me, I'll have you know, Okay, so that's a few million other teenage girls and me! I was crazy about Donny and his brothers - a phase spanning roughly from the age of ten to fifteen.

For my brother the 'Puppy Love' era was a mixed blessing. In much the same way as I had clung to Grandpy Delderfield's coat tails as an infant, so I pursued my brother as I got a little older. I was desperate to be included and involved in everything he did – not to mention attempting to join him and his friends when they went out to create carnage. As you can imagine – his idea of fun and 'street credibility' amongst his friends simply didn't include a pesky little sister. Yeah, it was okay to shove me over the fence for the ball, or do things that would get me in to hot water – but that's what little sisters are for isn't it? He knew I wasn't scared to do anything for him, and he used it well. That said, for some years he could be a bully, it wasn't until much later, that I realised he was suffering from a similar treatment and no surprise that he passed it down the line to take it out on me. So, to his rescue came Donny Osmond and my best friend Karen. At last I left him alone. The flip side of course, was every passing moment he had to listen to Osmonds' music.

Martin cruelly dubbed Donny as 'Donkey Osmond' – and with the Osmonds' revival of the past few years (which incidentally has proved even more exciting to me in middle age), so the nickname was revived by Martin, much to my husband's delight.

Karen and I went from Northchurch primary school to different 'middle schools' – she was at Thomas Bourne, in Durrants Lane, Berkhamsted. That didn't in any way harm our friendship – if anything it strengthened it. We were together all through the holidays, and members of the Junior Church choir. We were also in the Girl Guides – but whereas Karen diligently acquired her badges, I really wanted fun more than anything. Like many girls, I had previously been a brownie and to this day can remember the swearing in verse 'I promise that I'll do my best to do my duty to God, to serve the queen and help other people and keep the brownie guide law'.

We also attended the youth club in Northchurch parish room, where I became quite good at table tennis. We enjoyed the discos, although I couldn't dance for toffee and my second-hand clothes were really frightful. Still, the robust person I had become helped me through any further embarrassment, although it did mask a very sensitive side to my nature, which many may have missed – buried deep beneath my bravado - I craved acceptance.

Summer holidays were brilliant. So long as mum and dad knew where I was and who I was with, I got a fair amount of freedom – I soon learned that if you didn't flout the rules, then you could enjoy yourself far more.

I spent a lot of time at Karen's – indulging in her mum's fantastic lemon meringue pie. We camped out in her garage and our back garden – although a big spider that decided to seek refuge in the tent caused us to scream the place down one night – with dad hurtling outside to see what all the fuss was about. Mum supplied us with endless rounds of marmite on toast and I educated Karen with my Osmonds World magazines. Very soon she too was hooked – much to the chagrin of her brother Ian, who held me personally responsible.

One day when Karen and Ian came to tea, Ian had to ask mum to move the underwear from the line which was set up in the living room as a clothes airer. I think mum's not so 'smalls' on the line put him off his food!

I remember being really jealous of Karen when she broke her arm – her mum bought her a new Osmonds album – I was green with envy, although didn't want the plaster cast or pain to go with it of course. One snowfall we went tobogganing in the fields above St Mary's Avenue where she lived. My sledge failed to stop on the slope and I crashed headlong into the fence and barbed wire at the bottom of the field. Her younger brother Gary thought it highly amusing.

I was a bit calamity prone at times – like the time I had a go on Guy Holliday's bike – with its chunky wheels, but I didn't master the brakes and split my knee open on a pile of flint-stones on the verge. I kept splitting the same knee open for some time after – falling over in the road at Ashley Green when mum and dad took us to the firework display.

I sprained an ankle at middle school, which broke my heart as I couldn't attend the Christmas disco. Then at senior school on an amazing ice slide I collided with another girl and was knocked unconscious – remaining so for an hour and a half. That wasn't so bad as it got me out of a District schools cross-country race, which I'd been dreading. Apart from that though I have been very lucky in life, especially considering the risks I took in my endeavour to impress my brother.

One thing I never escaped from was the terror of the dentists. Martin had needed a brace for two years. I got away with that, but had an overcrowded mouth and had several trips to have double teeth removed. How I loathed going. I hated the gas, and the large black rubber stopper that kept your mouth open as well as the impatient dentist who had no tolerance with 'scared children'. The only flip side was having fish fingers and beans for tea – being soft enough to manage with a numb mouth and a comic or small gift from mum in commiseration. It's little wonder that I have been scared evermore of the dentist's chair – regressing to being a real baby when faced with the drill.

Being poorly was the only occasion I received ad hoc treats. There wasn't the money for any more, and having heard the words "Not today, love" and "No" so many times, I learned never to ask for anything.

The house at 3 Dell Road, as I've said before was cold and damp – it was as cold as Gaza, any day. The toilet of the house was by the front door – freezing, with a seemingly never ending flow of water streaming down the lower walls in winter. There was no toilet upstairs, so if in the night you needed to relieve yourself, it was no picnic. You'd try desperately to get back to sleep hoping the urge would go away. Invariably you'd give in, run to the loo and back again – but it was too late – by the time you were back in bed you were frozen solid and wide awake.

The kitchen was to the side of the house – we had a few replacement panes of glass – the result of over-exuberant ball games. The front room was at one time not in use – a bit like the posh front room of Gaza. We spent most of our time – certainly in school years, in the living room – dining room/come sitting room. We had a coal fire, and at Christmas dad would light the fire in the front room too – to air it. However, as we had no refrigerator (did we ever need one I ask?) it was easier for dad to keep one room cold for food preservation. Milk bottles stood in buckets of water. We didn't have a washing machine either - it would have made life much easier for mum – who hand-washed everything from dad's decorators' whites, to Martin's muddy football kit and my hockey and cross-country kit – how she coped I just don't know. The washing machine didn't surface until many years later, when in truth she had far less need for it – and by which time her red hands and knobbled knuckles were sore.

There was an under-stairs cupboard – dark and a dingy with a few too many cobwebs – where everything from sacks of potatoes, to tins of paint, tools and kindling wood were stored. The landing was a large open space where any heat generated soon dissipated.

Upstairs there were three bedrooms and the bathroom – equally freezing. We wore more clothes in bed than out of it in winter. Condensation froze on the inside of the windows and a hot water bottle was an essential accessory for us all. In winter moving away from the coal fire was a thing of dread. No sooner than you turned your back than the chill hit you. Poor mum wore more layers of clothes than I owned. She always felt the cold (mind you so did I) and I'm sure people must have thought her to be three clothes sizes bigger than she really was. As a young girl her father called her 'plate rack' as she was so skinny – thank God for suet puddings putting some meat on her bones.

Dad, having been brought up in a financially poor environment was ever frugal. It became a standing joke with us that if you were watching a programme on television, or reading and dared to leave the room for the toilet or kitchen, you would return to discover that the television or light had been turned off. Similarly in spring or autumn, when it wasn't cold enough for a fire, he would put on the electric fire to take the chill off the room – one bar only mind! Much later we finally managed to convince dad to have central heating installed – but he never really got to grips with using it properly, being too scared of the high bills.

A favourite saying of dad's was "there's plenty of wear left in that yet". After Martin and I left the nest and set up our own homes, we could always rely on dad to have anything we were replacing indoors.

With dad being a painter and decorator it was a busman's holiday decorating at home – which I can fully understand. As we marvelled at the odd colours he used in places indoors, it transpired he often had a tin of this, or half a tin of that left over from a job, so rather than waste it, he would use it at home - it tickled us to bits. Poor mum was never going to get palatial surroundings at that time! Frugal though dad may have been – it was borne of a habit from birth – a hard one to break – but his generosity of spirit amply compensated.

As mentioned earlier at one time Martin and I shared a bedroom, until we were older - I then acquired the smaller room at the front leaving him in the larger back bedroom. That was, until he became fanatical about aircraft spotting, and thus I was turfed out of my room with its view across Northchurch Common – it just so happened the planes taking off from Luton airport emerged over the horizon there.

Christmas was always a special family time. Martin let the cat out of the bag that Father Christmas didn't really exist – although I disputed that – after all we'd seen him with our own eyes on the back of the Lions Club float that went by the back gate. In fact Martin had ridden with Santa all the way to The Limit caravan site at the end of Covert Road – and hadn't I (after hastily putting the red wellies on) chased along behind?

Dad used to put a sack at the bottom of our beds, although one Christmas he decided to leave them outside the door – this coincided with me dreaming that Santa had forgotten me. So when I woke and saw no sack I was horror-struck until its new location was revealed.

Presents varied – large items such as bicycles and dolls prams were always second-hand, but we never went without. The hammering things took from us it's as well they weren't brand new – although they were always in good condition. Dad came out with me teaching me to use my bike with its stabilisers. I was so chuffed, albeit very wobbly, when the stabilisers were removed for the first time.

Like most kids, I couldn't sleep well at Christmas – was far too excited and anxious to rip the wrapping paper to shreds. I wore my Sunday best clothes on Christmas Day. The living room was always warm with its fire going all day, and the food was sumptuous. We usually had chicken instead of turkey as both mum and dad preferred it. I really don't know how we managed to eat so much. We had mum's delicious sausage rolls mid-morning; the main dinner mid-day; fruit and sweets in the afternoon and cold meats and pickles at tea-time as well as fruit, Angel Delight and that wonderful Nestle sterilised cream. Both dad and I would have devoured it straight from the tin if left to our own devices. I loved Satsumas and Cox's apples, which were also just a Christmas-time treat. Dad was heard every year to say 'It's all got to go" – or more precisely "'S all gotta goo" – referring to the perishable foods, as we were relying on the chill of the house to preserve it.

I remember one occasion when the 'bird', as my dad would call it, was delivered by Mrs Bachelor – who also delivered our eggs. This year we did have turkey and the only one they had was much bigger than the one ordered, but we were allowed to have it for the same price. That was all very well, but we didn't have a roasting tin big enough, so mum had to hurriedly get a new one – even then it only just fitted in the oven, and had a singed tail as it was squashed right up against the oven door.

There was one year, which wasn't so good for me. I had decided to make presents for mum and dad – mum's was a peg-bag – I can't remember what dad's was supposed to be – either way I used awful masking tape and old clothes – to put it frankly they were shocking presents and ended up being totally unusable. I still cringe about this today and learned the valuable lesson that the real pleasure of Christmas comes from the giving as opposed to the receiving. There was another year, when dad decided he was going to save money, like some of his customers did, and abandoned the buying of presents. As a child this was impossible to understand and we ended up with a few presents from relatives in sympathy – but Lily of the Valley talc wasn't my idea of a fun present – despite the kindness with which it was given.

We may not have had all the material things that many of our friends had, but we were richly showered in love, time and care from mum and dad.

We had brilliant weekends, frequently going up the common with picnics, makeshift rounders bats and cricket gear and enjoyed a great game with Auntie Joan and Uncle Fred. We would always go for a long walk through the beautiful Ashridge forest, which was my favourite part - it was this that nurtured my love of the countryside. We used to go on a lot of outings with Joan and Fred, we spent many an afternoon in Verulam Park, St Albans combined with more walking. The old cliché 'the best things in life are free' is so very true. We laughed at Uncle Fred, who could be quite dour at times, something was always 'getting his goat' – especially the Government. His well used phrase "Bah, gives yer the pip" became legendary. We also spent a lot of time visiting stately homes – and apart from Claydon House, which stirred my interest in becoming a Florence Nightingale, these I found boring at a younger age. I have since developed an appreciation of antiques, especially furniture, although it is only admired from afar and I still can't distinguish between the genuine article and 'tat'.

We never went away on holiday until I was nine years old. Until this time we went out on daily coach trips – which, since neither mum nor I were good travellers, meant an endless stream of travel tablets (those horrible 'Quells') and queasiness. It must have been hell for mum as we left early, arrived home late, and she had the daily washing of our clothes to do as well as preparing food for the trips.

It was very exciting when our first proper holiday at a guest house in Bournemouth was booked. We were going in the June – that is, until Martin went down with chicken pox. Okay – well we still had a week to go for, until I caught it too. I can still see mum crying on the doorstep as she told her sister. We had to cancel the holiday, but thankfully they could fit us in for September and, as it turned out, we had much better weather than we would have had in June. Mum cried when we had to come home – I guess things were really tough on her – it's not until you look back that you realise the sacrifices she made for us kids.

Dad was good with us too, giving us plenty of his time. We enjoyed burying him in the sand and holding his hand in the sea. Neither mum nor dad liked the beach, but as with most parents, they tolerated it for our sakes. Dad made me a pair of stilts when they were all the rage. Sadly, he couldn't make a space-hopper or pogo stick! He took us fishing along the Grand Union canal at nearby Dudswell. Martin had a real rod, I had a bamboo cane which dad made up for me.

Mum took us to catch tadpoles in the River Bulbourne armed with our nets and buckets. We were so lucky having parents whom always took such an interest in us. I wouldn't have swapped my childhood for anything.

Auntie Joan used to come over from Chesham every week to Gramps – cleaning windows etc to help out. I used to like her visits as she always bought us a Crunchie bar! Poor Auntie

Joan - she had obviously forgiven Gramps for drowning her kittens when she was a little girl. Apparently they had a cat for catching vermin. When it miraculously produced a litter of kittens, Joan was thrilled. Gramps was not amused - they didn't need any more mouths to feed, so he did the practical thing and drowned them in the water butt. I can just imagine Joan's distress - I don't think I would have spoken to him for weeks!

The only pets we had were a couple of hamsters - Soda and Suky, and Snowy the rabbit. Snowy was stolen by a fox one Saturday night, and beside myself with upset, it was another Sunday school day I was given licence to miss. Don't be misled - once I was a bit older and in the Junior Church I never missed a week, and enjoyed it immensely.

My hamster Soda, was a clever little thing - she could climb the stairs. One day she got out and went missing. We later found her behind mum and dad's wardrobe. I remember well the fateful day when she died. Mum - who hated all things small and furry, had to remove her from the cage - rigid as a board - that's both mum and Soda I think! She did a grand job of burying her before I got home from school.

I don't recall exactly when dad bought his first car, except that I went with him to collect it. It was a blue Ford Zephyr with a long bench seat in the front. While we had a blue car, my cousins had a pink one - in the days when pastel shades seemed very 'hip'. Dad was so pleased with it. He was a frightful driver - you felt every gear change and movement. Mum describes him as being very 'jerky' - no wonder she got car sick so easily.

I always associate Princes Risborough in Buckinghamshire with a Sunday trip out with Auntie Joan and Uncle Fred. The fan belt went while passing through the town. A lady kindly gave us all cold drinks while we waited for help. I don't know if we called out someone to do repairs, or if a pair of tights was offered as a temporary remedy.

The Zephyr was turned in when dad was offered a Morris Minor van from Ellis & Son, his employers. The firm was closing and dad went self-employed. The van came as a good deal so naturally he made use of it. Sundays out were never quite the same. The paint and solvent fumes added to my nausea. Bar mum and dad, we all piled in the back sitting on cushions. At that time Ashby Road, Northchurch was an unmade road, with a heavy camber and potholes – we always knew when we were nearly home by the angle of the van. That van went on forever – until just before dad took early retirement in fact. We went everywhere in it – holidays, day trips and to Tring fish and chip shop – when dad seemed to exceed land-speed records to get home before the food had chance to cool.

Dad always seemed to encourage the van to go faster – leaning forward at the wheel. My cousin, Sharon, reminded me of a phrase dad used a lot when driving – he would frequently say 'gently Bentley', while trying to manoeuvre through heavy traffic. The rest of the time he would refer to the van as the 'jalopy'.

My biggest adventure was a school trip, courtesy of The Augustus Smith School - a week on the Isles of Scilly. Augustus Smith, a Berkhamsted squire and banker, leased the islands from 1834 and lived there from 1853 until his death in 1872. He was involved in what was known as the 'Battle of Berkhamsted Common' in 1866, when he fought Lord Brownlow who had enclosed the land.

I was twelve years old and it was my first time away from home and my parents. I was so excited about it I didn't have time to get homesick. In fact I couldn't understand some of my classmates getting tearful at all, there was so much to see and do – much fun to be had, and certainly plenty of distractions. It taught me to stand on my own to feet and to make the most of new opportunities and discoveries. I revelled in it.

Getting there took an age, having to get a train into London, then another one to Penzance – a long journey even by rail. The most exciting aspect was taking the Sikorsky helicopter across from Penzance to the heliport on St. Mary's island. It was the first time I'd flown in any capacity, and after initial apprehension I was enthralled – and still am by the very act of flying. The view across the entire range of the islands as we turned on our approach was simply spectacular. I will never forget the experience. The islands are so very pretty. We went in April time, when the flora really begins to flourish. Being in the Gulf Stream means everything comes early there and fortunately for us we had some very warm sunshine. We stayed in a youth hostel type building on the island of Bryher.

I loved the fact that we had to go from island to island by boat. There were old churches to explore and a plethora of seabirds, including puffins. Each island has something different to offer – the gorgeous sandy beaches at St Martin's and the lighthouse at St Agnes with a sandbar joining it to the small island of Gugh, accessible only at low tide. Tresco had the magnificent Abbey, gardens and Valhalla museum and St Mary's was the main island, with more hotels, commerce and inhabitants. Bryher had the marvellous Hell Bay – with its wild rocky promontories. It was exhilarating standing on the rocks being lashed by rain or waves with the wind blowing fit to knock you sideways.

The walking was brilliant and we had fun in all we did, even brass rubbings and rock pool transepts. We watched the gig race, which was held weekly. Each island had its representative boat - we had to shout for Czar – presumably this being connected to Bryher. I can't recall where it came – but don't think it won, even with our support.

Unfortunately we couldn't take a planned trip to the Bishop Rock lighthouse, due to the rough seas, but we did get a boat trip closer to the islands. It was really choppy – you can quite understand why the surrounding seabed is something of a graveyard for shipwrecks. We got to see more of the puffins and other birds at closer quarters – although I was a bit dubious when some of the boys tried tipping the boat – it wouldn't have taken much to turn us over that's for sure!

My tomboy lifestyle developed into a love of sports and I enjoyed racing about the hockey field with a vengeance. I hated netball, as there wasn't enough space to run around the court, preferring the rougher field sports. I also came to quite enjoy athletics and cross-country running - making sure I ran through the puddles instead of around them (poor mum - all that hand-washing).

It was at middle school, I learned a lot about people - that being nice sometimes makes you a target for bullies. I was brought up to be polite and kind to people. In those days, I hadn't really developed my father's short fuse - that came much later. Despite my hardy, robustness in the sporting arena, I was meek in nature. Like mum, I wouldn't cause arguments (except those with my brother, of course), preferring to walk away from any unpleasant situations - that also changed drastically later in life!

Most days I was given a lift to school with Deborah, who lived in Northchurch too. She seemed to think it was okay to make me carry her bags home from school, threatening no more lifts in her wake. I couldn't be bothered to argue, so duly obliged - like a doormat. She always picked on me when we played a game of 'British Bulldog' in the playground - seeking only to catch me. She was sneaky with her bullying, only visibly nasty when we were alone, although others guessed what she was doing. My friend Janet's mum would only allow one child at a time in to play with her. Deborah knew this and living nearby, she would often see me going to Janet's and race along to catch me up, knowing I would be turned away from seeing my friend.

It was all childish stuff but most hurtful at the time, and I was eternally grateful when I got to Ashlyns, my senior school, and away from her. I'm sure she's a much nicer person now, but as a ten-thirteen year old she was simply horrid.

Aged eleven, one day I let Wendy borrow my crayons. Some of the other girls in the class told me I was mad, I shouldn't do it - I wouldn't get them back - as Wendy's family were always in trouble with the police. Wendy had done me no harm, and she gratefully returned them when she was finished with them. I went from being accepted as a nice person, to be picked on by cruel childishness. This didn't materialise into anything more until I attended Ashlyns.

For some reason a group of girls didn't like me – I don't know why - I enjoyed school, worked hard and kept my nose clean. Maybe I was a 'goody-two-shoes' to them - it's a mystery to me. A nasty piece of work called Sally joined the clan, and took delight in throwing stones at me as I walked home from school. Thankfully we went in different directions after a short walk, but even so, it was intimidating and spiteful. I was lucky that only my pride was wounded, but I did reap some reward a couple of years or so later. I had joined Hertfordshire police cadets and was in Tesco getting milk for the shift. As I got to the check-out who should be on the till, but Sally. She eyed my uniform up beneath my jacket and, oh so sweetly, asked how I was, saying how lovely it was to see me! I smiled politely, saying nothing, just looking. As I left the shop I wanted to whoop with delight. At last – one up to me. She'd obviously thought I was now in a bigger, tougher 'gang' than hers – or maybe she'd finally started to grow up.

Before I got to Ashlyns, during the summer of 1975 Karen and her mum had a real surprise for me. They had got tickets for us to go and see The Osmonds at Earls Court. I was beside myself with excitement. I couldn't keep still at the prospect. Wowee! We set about making our own rosettes, and I embroidered (in amazingly neat stitching) D O N N Y at an angle down one of my trouser legs. The day came and lives with me forever. Both Karen and I agreed we didn't think we'd be able to scream. We were way near the back, but the big screens helped us see our idols. Donny came out in a puff of pink smoke dangled on a wire over the audience. Couldn't scream? – We were like banshees – demented screeching teenagers in love. I had a woman next to me who was obviously there under sufferance – well I admit it was noisy! I received a look that would freeze hell over when I accidentally collided with her whilst brandishing my scarf. The music and performance was simply stunning – a truly professional well orchestrated programme – and above all, they were there – my heroes and future husband (in my dreams again). The only thing to mar the evening was on the train ride home when a disgustingly drunk man was sick – some of which fell on Karen's long blonde hair – it was absolutely repulsive and I can smell the acrid vomit even now.

These past three years have seen a revival of The Osmond Brothers group and Donny separately as a solo artist. For me Donny was always my favourite Osmond, but I prefer listening to the group as a whole. Having seen both Donny and the Osmond Brothers twice since their revival, I can say they are all they ever were to me – it's even better as a middle-aged woman.

Yes, we still scream between records, but more greatly appreciate the music and their personal qualities than we did in the seventies – and of course, we've matured a tad. The last concert I went to was The Osmond Brothers on 16th March 2006 at The Apollo, Hammersmith. Now that was the best, most enjoyable concert I have ever been to. It was filmed and to my delight my sister-in-law, Julie and I are on the DVD - I have relived the show a million times over - it was simply awesome! I have the undisputed pleasure of seeing Donny again in concert later this year - another date for the diary!

My days at Ashlyns were thoroughly enjoyable. The building had been a foundling hospital in wartime. Mum, as a child, remembers the children together in the town, clad in their brown uniforms. One of my classrooms was the former nursery – with yellow tiles on the wall, depicting baby rabbits and ducks etc. It has an impressive separate chapel that was used for assemblies. The grounds of the school were fantastic - extensive, with great sports fields, tennis courts and wonderful trees. Lazy summer lunch breaks were spent lying on the grass chatting, or walking round the perimeter of the grounds.

It was fabulous luck that Karen and I were put in the same form – a coincidence I'm sure, but fortuitous none the less. We were in different stream classes for lessons, but at least we got to be together at other times.

Ashlyns was a great school for me. It taught you to be independent and gave you a fair amount of freedom. However, this was only good if you were adult enough to appreciate that freedom and not abuse it – as many found to their cost. In truth you could also take or leave education to some degree. You could achieve well, or be lazy – either way, people didn't seem to be pulled up much for not working.

I enjoyed learning – worked hard and played hard. I ran cross-country for the school and athletics – although I have to say that I didn't always enjoy these activities. I got so incredibly nervous before a run, my stomach knotted with fear – it somewhat detracted from my enjoyment – hence why the accident on the ice was something of a relief in one way. I also played tennis for the school – being paired with Karen. Philippa Newland and Jo Brown were the top pairing, with Karen and me second. We had many a good game with them. I had a bit of a temper on the court – getting frustrated with myself more than anything else. I had an 'all or nothing' serve – I hit a ball so hard that it was either an ace or fault! Jo was an excellent player but fiercely aggressive with it.

My biggest sporting achievements, however, came as a member of the school hockey team. In reality I was surprised to get picked. I don't think I was initially a good player, rather, I was chosen for the sheer effort, energy and enthusiasm I displayed. As it happened my skills greatly improved and I broke many hockey sticks through the sheer power of my hit. The team had amazing spirit and we were each dedicated and determined to a fault.

I shall never forget when we won the District final against Tring School – who were a good side. We were playing at home and the rain came down in stair-rods. The mud was up to our knees, not conducive to a skilful game, and our victory was decided by the grit, guts and attitude of us as a unit. It was a brilliant result – we were so thrilled.

I can't possibly mention sport at Ashlyns without mentioning Ann Lobban – our sports mistress. A big lady – nay, an Amazon is what we thought – she wasn't one to argue with. That said she was a very kind person when you got to know her. She came across as ferocious and mean to the new third year pupils – me included until I knew better. I was lucky I was both good at sport and interested in it. For those who made no effort at all – she would have been someone to avoid. Ann Lobban taught us all the values of effort and sportsmanship. I remember specifically a tournament we were playing in. We had just played our last match in the group and were waiting to see the result of an ongoing match that would decide our fate – in particular whether we would get through to the next round or be homeward bound on the bus.

Of course, we knew which result we needed so started to cheer for the side who could take us through. Ann Lobban went ballistic! I had never seen her so angry in my life – how dare we cheer a side just because we wanted another team to lose – how unsporting and ungracious we were! Oh boy – we learned the error of our ways – and of course, she was absolutely right. As it happened I can't remember the outcome of the match at all – just the well deserved lesson we took with us. I applaud you Ann Lobban – you have my utmost respect. Womanhood started to kick in for me at fourteen years old, one Christmas time – on Boxing Day while we were at Nanny and Grandpy Sear's to be exact. This gripping pain across my stomach was what mum had warned me to be on the lookout for. I dashed home and got out the contraptions mum had bought for me in readiness.

I remember when I was nine years old she given instruction on how to use the sanitary belt and pads – I hoped I'd get the hang of it so to speak! As if all this wasn't embarrassing enough, I was mortified, when for years mum made surreptitious nightly checks of my 'undies' – as she waited for 'it' to arrive.

While I was quite prepared for the unpleasant monthly curse, neither I, nor mum and dad I imagine, were ready for my pre-menstrual tension – something which reared its ugly head in varying degrees from bad to awful. I found my 'bouncing' hormones dictated my emotions. There would be fits of temper followed by deep contrition – or floods of tears and feeling sorry for myself. Mum at least received regular flowers from me by way of apology for being so awkward. Dad could exacerbate me with ease at such times and both being stubborn, we would lock horns frequently - I would spoil for an argument then burst into tears at the drop of a hat.

For anyone who has never suffered with 'PMT' it is hard to explain. It is like a red mist that forms behind the eyes. Rationality goes out of the window. I can appreciate how women do stupid things at this time – it is nigh on impossible to focus on what you are doing. The crazy thing is, when the 'curse' finally arrives, it is as if a storm cloud has lifted. You cannot believe you are the same person. It is about this time that the deep sense of guilt comes in to play. It is a most wretched experience, and took me many, many years to find something that really helped to alleviate this. Having passed into womanhood as it were, I was then getting my head down towards my 'O' Levels and thinking about my future in the working world.

When I was eight I wanted to be one of three things – a nurse (no surprise there), a policewoman, or a nun! Don't ask me where the nun idea came from – suffice to say I'm glad I didn't pursue it.

Florence Nightingale had inspired my nursing tendencies and the Police had always intrigued me. Was it the occasion when Martin and a group of boys got in a bit of bother – nothing bad – just a bit of over exuberant youthfulness that warranted a quiet word from the local police? I gaped at them in awe. Then two of Martin's friends – his best mate Ian, and Steve Wheatley, joined Hertfordshire Police cadets. I found out a bit more about the cadets and then sent off for information about the progression into the police force. That was that – my mind was made up – the police force was what I wanted.

The big wide world beckoned - little did I know how quickly I would discard those 'rose coloured glasses' of mine.

CHAPTER 4

FROM BABY BLUE...

"**I**'ve got in, I've got in!" I came screaming through the front door having just borrowed Nanny's phone to call Hertfordshire Constabulary. I had just been told I had been awarded a place in the police cadets and would be starting in September 1978.

I was over the moon. Earlier in the year I had attended County Police Headquarters at Welwyn Garden City to sit an entrance exam, for group participation exercises, physical exercise tests and medical examinations, followed by facing an interview panel. It was quite a rigorous process, taking two days to complete. I had been strangely relaxed about it all – maybe it was meant to be. They hadn't taken any cadets the previous year, so I was one of thirty-two accepted from a field of over three hundred applicants. I was elated.

The first thing I needed to do in preparation for entry to the world of the police cadets was to master the female use of 'tampons' – I couldn't be having to deal with the contraptions I was currently employing – especially with so much physical exercise being on the agenda. Thankfully the transition went smoothly – what a bonus – how women coped without them I will never know.

So while happily passing my 'O' levels that summer I was in a perpetual state of excitement about my new career. Some of my teachers weren't happy, preferring that I stay on and take 'A' levels, then go to university.   Others, like Ann Lobban, were delighted with my success and wished me well. As I look around me now, I still see many youngsters gaining 'A' levels and university degrees, without having the first idea of what to do with their lives. One particular friend of mine took three degree-courses back to back – a perennial student. She must have been approaching thirty years old before thinking about earning a living! I guess I was lucky – I knew what I wanted to do and was fortunate enough to be able to do it.

The first Sunday in September 1978 arrived and mum and dad ferried me to Police Headquarters, which was to be my home for the next 'school year'.   I guess I must have been somewhat nervous although I don't truly recall it. There were twenty-two cadets in total in our class, the other ten were in a different group as they were effectively a school year older than the rest of us, so they had a different itinerary and were seconded to police stations sooner.

There was a fierce curriculum of physical training, academic studies, learning drill, discipline and generally growing up. There was self-defence training, life saving, first aid and an outward-bound course.

It was a strange, but very proud feeling to don a 'police' uniform – albeit the cadet uniforms rightly had a flash on each shoulder indicating that you were only a cadet – with a blue band worn on the hat or cap.

It is important to differentiate between cadets, special constables, traffic wardens and regular police officers, so that the public knows whom they are talking to. In practice I'm afraid it doesn't really work – people generally see a 'uniform' and think 'police' not understanding there are different roles, skill areas and responsibilities within the organisation. Thus, very often their expectations are quite unrealistic, which in turn can lead to frustration, confusion and resentment. I imagine the same is true today with Police Community Support Officers who do not have the same powers as police officers and suffer bad press through no fault of their own.

Without digressing too far ahead, I know none of us cadets will ever forget those first two weeks. We were given so much physical exercise that we could scarcely put one foot in front of the other each night. The lactic acid was impossible to shift. We worked one set of muscles after the other and felt like we were dying.

Come 7 a.m. each day there was morning PT. Now depending on who supervised us would dictate whether we got wet in the pool, sent for a run, or were doing sprints and press-ups face down in the snow followed by circuit training in the gym. Personally I always hoped it would be a run, as this was my strongest area. For me a run was just one continuous exercise - when you crossed the line the pain was over – unlike the other activities when the start-stop process was infinitely repetitive and more debilitating.

Staff Collantine was the main gym instructor – with a nickname for every cadet – I was known as 'Deldy' derived from Delderfield. This later evolved into Delders and Dels amongst other, far ruder names!

Our swimming instructor was Brian Waters – known as 'Muddy'. Muddy was ferocious with his training sessions, and positively dreaded for morning PT. One particular morning, one of the older cadets – a non-swimmer, refused to jump in the pool. We all were made to wait until she obeyed him. She still refused to jump. Muddy ordered us to go and change into our gym kit and he took us for a punishing circuit training session. We then had to change back into swimming kit and get back in the pool. Then he had us doing drill in full uniform. This was all between seven and eight a.m. - and still the cadet refused to jump in. I can't remember now how it ended – did she get pushed in?

I was a mid-stream swimmer but even so found Muddy to be a 'swine' when sending us off on endless lengths of the pool. He put the slowest in first so that the fast swimmers had to swim over you to get by – which resulted in frequent duckings and the consumption of half a gallon of chlorine. If nothing else it certainly made me a stronger swimmer. Life saving training was all part of the routine and most of us came away with our 'bronze medallions'.

I remember during circuit training one day, Michelle, thankfully a very petite girl, slipped off the wall bars. She was right near the top – we all gasped in horror as she fell, trying in vain to grab a passing bar.

Thank heavens for Chris Saunders, who managed to get beneath her and catch her before she came to grief. We were worked really hard and with aching limbs and perspiring hands it is little wonder more people didn't fall from those wall bars, or indeed the top of the ropes. Funny how one fleeting thought instantly conjures up another memory!

The ropes – I'll never forget Ann Davis (known as Dave) - a gentle-natured person with a perpetual smile and the physical strength of an ox. She had no technique on the ropes at all and never mastered how to use her feet to ease her climb. She is the only person I have ever seen climb the ropes using nothing but the power in her arms - and boy were they powerful.

Running was something I was good at, despite the fact I never enjoyed it. I relished the shower at the end, and that wonderful feeling of being fit, but contrary to popular belief – I never found it easy. Just because I was good at it didn't make it a stroll in the park – in fact I
pushed myself even harder to try and beat the guys so it hurt all the more.

There are so many wonderful memories of that first year and some other chores that weren't so good. We had to box our beds each day – an old army ritual as I understand it – you had to fold all your bedding and make it into a neat box with the counterpane wrapped around the outside. We had room inspections daily, so you couldn't afford to slip up. Towards the end of the year a few did cheat by using their sleeping bags and leaving the 'box' ready for inspection. We could only get away with that nearer to our passing out parade, but it was worth the occasional try.

Drill was good fun, but the uniforms weren't the easiest to keep well pressed. We had a best uniform, which invariably stayed as immaculate as possible, with creases as near to razor sharp as they could be. Boots and shoes had to be 'bulled' until they shone like glass – I actually found that quite therapeutic. I remember one parade when a girl, 'Frankie' had upset one of the guys and he unkindly trod on her foot destroying the hours of work she'd put into her shoes.

Like any drill squad, there is always one person at least who cannot march for toffee. A couple suffered from having two left feet to begin with, but they got there in the end. There are always amusing moments that spring to mind - like when Inspector Cox tripped over when he came to inspect some Probationer Police Constables. We were lined up behind the group of officers and soon found out that sniggering was not going to be tolerated – we got well and truly roasted and discovered that once again we had a touch more growing up to do.

As part of our training in the April we had an outward-bound course in Snowdonia – we had to reach peak fitness as the walking was to be arduous. We wore heavy walking boots for circuit training and on runs – to strengthen our legs. The party of girls went first, with the boys going after we'd returned - it was the only time we were segregated by gender.

As the bus circled preparing to leave headquarters, so the fellas stood at a window, holding their caps to their chests while strains of the beautiful 'Nielsen' track 'Without You' boomed out at us. It was a great moment and I think we realised life was more fun with the fellas around.

As the course progressed so meal times became a right pain with regular bitchy episodes – non-stop moaning and comments like "Get your own" were frequently heard. I had little tolerance for that aspect at all - I guess that's the trouble with having all girls together – I'm sure if the fellas had been there, some of the girls would have behaved better, if only to impress!

Each morning started with a constitutional jog to the mountain stream for ablutions. The water was icy cold. We had to wash in the stream and weren't allowed out until our heads had been fully submerged at least three times. I thought I would never complain about being cold ever again. That said – your body literally tingled and glowed after you alighted from the stream. The heat coursed through your veins and you felt totally cleansed. It became an enjoyable ritual for the 'afterglow' alone.

We had an overnight trek and set up our tents at the base of the mountains – this we did in poor weather and high winds, after first dragging a dead sheep from a stream, to prevent pollution of the water. We had a howling snowstorm that night and some of the girls were unable to put their boots on the following morning as they had frozen. That, disappointingly, cut short our trek. Most of us could have continued, but the team leaders, of which I was one, agreed that we should stick together.

We learned that we had to work to the weakest in the group – both in terms of walking ability, and in the event of apparatus problems. Thus, having found a small cottage we managed to make a telephone call to our instructors who came to our rescue with the minibus.

I soon discovered that I had a weakness with certain heights. I was okay rock climbing on the way up, but not so clever on the way down – it almost gave me a touch of vertigo. I progressed and had a good go at a particular climb but couldn't completely eradicate that feeling of vulnerability.

I fell in love with Snowdonia – the walking and scenery was magnificent. I have always been enthralled by mountains – they are omnipotent to me. They are daunting by dusk – the shadow rising into the sky above your head feels quite menacing, yet by day – to walk high into their midst puts you on top of the world. I have always felt that a person of no faith at all could not fail to feel the existence of some 'power' or 'greater being' beyond them when standing on a mountain peak.

We scaled Snowdon – taking the hard route – the ridge path. It was in the early stages of the hike that we were grateful for the training we had undergone – as we climbed interminable steep rocky paths. Nearer the top at one point it was so foggy we could only see the feet in front of us. It was fortuitous that we had heavy backpacks keeping us rooted to the ground in the strong wind.

We crossed a ridge with sheer drops either side – the fog was at that point most welcome! Apart from the sense of achievement and a delicious Mars bar as we reached the summit – the top was a real anti-climax. There was a snack bar (shut at that time of the year) with litter strewn around. What a disgraceful greeting after such a wonderful journey! As we descended the other side of the mountain, the fog lifted, blessing us with the kiss of sunshine. The views were spectacular and life never felt so good.

My hair became legendary throughout our stay – with no hairdryer my hair turned into a mass of unruly waves and curls – ably assisted by breezy conditions. I couldn't have cared less about my appearance – I was in a state of perpetual elation , at one with nature.

Towards the end of our first year we passed our exams and finished on a high with pride at our passing out parade and gymnastics display. I was grateful to win the Academic Cup and Cross Country trophy – but above all I had thoroughly enjoyed myself. I don't remember any bad times – I'm sure there were a few, but most insignificant if indeed they existed. Some of the girls teamed up as best mates, but while I was closer to some than others, in the main I liked to feel I was everyone's friend. I remember each person in some special way (albeit some for being plain bitchy) but on the whole we all gelled as a unit.

There were some great characters, the biggest being Chris Saunders – a small, stocky-framed guy with a wicked sense of fun and devilment. He could be utterly infuriating at times but we all loved him dearly.

During the summer holiday that ensued, together with my friend Karen Till, I had a week-long secondment helping the Red Cross at Hertford – giving disabled children and young adults a holiday. This was a new, enlightening experience. Karen and I then took off to the Canary Islands for two weeks, relishing my first ever aeroplane flight.

As a second year (senior) cadet time was spent at the local police station, attached to a shift – this being until you reached the ripe old age of eighteen-and-a-half and could join the rank and file of the regular police force. One day a week was spent back at Police Headquarters, the rest of the time you fell into the routine of shifts really getting to learn what police work was all about.

On my first day, I walked from home to Berkhamsted Police Station in smart, full uniform (I didn't realise I could wear a civilian jacket over the top at that time). I found it strange when people I didn't know said hello to me – wearing a uniform in public was a new experience, but one that I soon got very used to.

I arrived at the station to be greeted by a dour man who seemed unimpressed with the arrival of a 'gadget' - as cadets were known to the regular officers. I soon found out that Malcolm was often grumpy but it didn't help ease the 'first-day' nerves.

The Shift on duty was Group Four and they had the dubious honour of fitting me into their number. The Sergeant, Frank Manfield was reputed to have little time for female officers in those days. Although I was only a cadet, I like to think I went some way to changing his opinions and I had an absolute ball on his shift. He was not one to be crossed and he commanded respect. All the guys worked hard and played hard – and boy were the Christmas parties good!

I learned from Martyn to wear my uniform with pride and to be diligent in everything I did. Stuart got me thinking about what we were looking for when patrolling streets at night. He also taught me how to act in public order situations and although I did well assisting him in one fracas, I quickly discovered how 'not to give evidence' in court!

After playing into the defence solicitor's hand, I soon learned that giving evidence meant adhering to the evidence only. Any little comments or additional words could be picked up on and exploited. I felt that I had let Stuart down and vowed this would never happen again. I fared much better on my next appearance in the witness box and thankfully took this with me throughout my career.

Alan drove the 'Area car' - which later became known as the 'Instant Response car'. I loved the way he dealt with awkward drivers. On one occasion when a motorist was incredibly rude to him, Alan was polite beyond reproach. He then set about reporting the driver for several offences and left him with a smile and 'Have a nice day, Sir'. Of course had the man been congenial himself, he would only have received words of caution. It was a clever policy and one I sought to replicate. If people are abusive and disrespectful towards you then they have no right to expect any in return. That said – a police officer needs to be polite and courteous at all times, no matter how great the level of duress or provocation.

I have heard so many people complaining at police officers with comments such as 'Haven't you got anything better to do?' - if only the public realised that such remarks can be like waving a red rag at a bull. Most officers seek to be fair at all times – especially as it is easy, in particular for motorists, to commit minor transgressions. A word of warning at such times is always the best policy – unless of course, someone is blatantly rude. There is a rule-book and suffice to say it does get thrown at deserving cases!

Adjusting my body to shift work was another learning curve. After my first night shift I didn't know whether I was punch-drunk or counter-sunk. I was hellishly tired but also incredibly hungry. I found sleep during the day was very hard to come by but gradually adapted. Of course, the Monday's back at headquarters didn't really help me to get into the full swing of things - that came later.

After a lazy summer break I found my fitness levels had dropped and I had some catching up to do. I took myself out running at home and being blessed by the Chiltern Hills and steep inclines up Northchurch Common I actually became fitter than ever. Gradually I found I could beat more of the male cadets than before and was thrilled when I came third in the National Police Cadet cross Country Championships at Tally-Ho, Birmingham the following April.

I still had much growing up to do during my time at Berkhamsted. One particular detective, Tom, who was full of little comments and innuendos, could make me turn beetroot red with consummate ease. I had to grow out of my embarrassing blushing phase. It took a while, but I gradually won the day. I learned to give as good as I got with banter and to stand up for myself. This may sound obvious – but I was still only just eighteen years old – and very naïve at that, so the quicker I learned, the better shape I would be in by the time I became a regular officer.

In meal breaks on night shift we might have a game of nomination whist. I became renowned for putting my foot in it with remarks that had innuendo capacity. One such occasion was during a game, when Malcolm, who had been on a winning streak, started losing. My innocent observation "I've noticed this about you Malcolm – you always start strongly, then wilt towards the end" provoked much hilarity. I made many more – far worse comments than that, of course, but I am glad to have provided some fun and entertainment. Any time I bump into Frank Manfield he delights in reminding me of those 'good old days'.

I had a month-long secondment during my senior cadetship, in January 1980 - this time to the Cheshire Home in Hitchin – helping the carers and auxiliary nurses with the diverse group of physically and mentally handicapped residents.

Here was I – a naïve eighteen-year old from a fairly sheltered upbringing ready to embark on another part of character building and personal development. I was terrified! I had never been around physically or mentally handicapped people before and didn't know what to expect. I arrived amid the chaos of lunchtime, which did nothing to ease the nerves, boost my confidence or whet my appetite!

Before long I found my way about and settled in. I got to know the residents, who varied from people with physical or mental handicaps, to a combination of both. Some of the people had been born with their handicaps while others had acquired them through illness or accidents later on in life.

There were a mix of characters - people like Frank, who was confined to a wheelchair after an accident, but was upbeat and a laugh a minute. Susan was in the latter stages of Multiple Sclerosis and bed-bound - a tough call, and so difficult on her husband and young child who came to visit. Then there was Keith, a young spastic, quadriplegic, who whizzed about on his electric chair.

Keith was pivotal in teaching me about handicap. With an easy chuckle he was full of life and happiness. He had a machine on the tray of his chair and a band round his head with a long arm attached to it. Using the arm he pressed the keys of the machine - which were akin to a computer keyboard. As he spelled out words so the machine spoke them out loud (with an American accent). This was the only way in which he could communicate fully with you. We got to discussing music, which he loved - like me he was more interested in the lyrics of songs, than the actual tunes.

One day Keith made me to follow him to his room, where he showed me his 'work'. He had written lyrics for songs - they were not just good, they were excellent. I felt deeply humbled. So severe were his handicaps that you could have been forgiven for not appreciating that his mind has more than compensated for any physical deficiencies. I had learned a valuable lesson. At the time the song 'Babe' by Styx was in the charts and it has forever linked me to a memory of Keith.

Years later, I got to know a work colleague, Brian, who has multiple sclerosis. He told me about the time he had spent in a wheelchair. I recall him telling me that when you are in a chair, people never speak to you. They address the carer or person pushing the chair, saying things like 'How is he?' It used to drive him mad - the chair was for his legs - there was nothing wrong with his ears or tongue! I'm sure my accountant, Bob, would agree - he may have no use of his arms and legs, but he has the sharpest brain of anyone I've ever met, and a keen sense of humour and wit to match.

My month at Cheshire Home changed my life for good - I had started to truly grow up and I came away knowing that I could never judge people by disability, or make assumptions from appearances alone. It was to stand me in good stead for the rigours of police work - but much more than that - it has taught me to see beyond handicap and appreciate the worth of every human being.

I have subsequently been to many police retirement or 'leaving' functions and invariably I find that ex-cadets speak fondly of this introduction to the police service.

Inspector Dick Cox had been in charge of the cadets for many years until his retirement. He was awarded an M.B.E for his service and I have never heard a bad word spoken about the man. Every cadet remembers him with great affection and respect.

I have no regrets whatsoever for not going into the Sixth Form at school or university. Joining the police cadets was a small step toward my degree course in the 'University of Life'! I found a police career to be one pretty swift way of growing up and although it made me somewhat cynical, it gave a balance to all things 'human'. To me there has been no better education than dealing with people – having to learn how to talk to others and appreciate that there are often many different sides to any argument or story.

Good interpersonal skills are essential – together with exercising discretion, compassion, sensitivity, tolerance, firmness and sound judgement at all times with the highest integrity.

Linda Pottinger

Sweet 16yrs - a police cadet    **Snowdonia course - Spring 1979**

Cadets' Passing Out Parade - July 1979 (I'm on the far right!)

My first day as a Police Constable

CHAPTER 5
TO CHEQUERED BAND

Hustle, bustle, push and shove, who will win the race?
Full steam ahead, the milling crowds
squeeze the life out of your face.

Don't stand still in case you fall to get trampled under feet,
And someone else will take the prize for what you all compete.

Why all the clamour and the din, the fighting and suppression,
Stress pulling folks apart to plunge them into depression?

I'm sure that God must feel so sad, for the man he did create -
Is hell bent on self-destruction - love diminishing through hate.

So much is missed within the rush, no pause to draw a breath,
And in the hordes a flying by there risks a lonely death.

If advice is not too late, we should stop to look about -
At faces cloaked in misery, eyes vacant, full of doubt.

Just what controls the lives they lead - is it money, fear or success?
Who knows, but they have hurried past their chance for happiness.

From the introduction as a Police cadet, here arrived the real world – doing the 'job' itself. I went to training school at Ryton on Dunsmore, near Coventry for ten weeks - something I viewed as a necessary evil.

After the police cadets I found training school to be something of a damp squib. The discipline was lax by comparison, the lessons were okay and informative and it was essential to pass the exams. There was a certain amount of drill and physical training, but it wasn't challenging. I did however meet some thoroughly decent people and that was its saving grace. Camaraderie is a big issue in the police service. You are one cog in a big organisation, but the empathy runs deep. If you consider that your work colleagues may one day 'save your life' on the street and that you may have to 'save theirs' you can understand why teamwork is so vital to its success.

You have to trust others and be trusted. It means you need courage when faced with adversity and an endless supply of common sense. Without these things a police career is unthinkable.

Having completed training school I was posted to Hemel Hempstead Police Station, Dacorum. I was lucky to be on a spirited shift with a good skipper who always got the balance right between praise and correction. He knew how to encourage you to develop and how to improve what you did.

I lived in a police house in Bennetts End, Hemel Hempstead, with two other police women (you were allowed to be called WPCs in those days – the job is now asexual – everyone is a PC!). One of the girls, Theresa, was on my shift and really looked after me – she is one of the loveliest, kindest people I've ever known. I stayed in the police house until I could drive - I then returned to live at home with mum, dad and Martin.

I spent much of my two-year probationary period walking the beat, only occasionally going out with another officer in a patrol car, until I took my police driving course. The walking was a good experience – you interacted with the public, froze on nights and got soaked frequently if you couldn't find shelter. At night you would creep about, rattling door handles as you went. On one occasion I was truly spooked – walking round the back of the shops in the Old High Street, checking premises were secure. It was a wet night, rain dripped from the gutters and it was pitch black. As I turned into a service area a cat leapt out at me from where it had been scavenging amongst the bins. I jumped out of my skin slamming my back into the wall nearby. The cat squawked in fright and flew off while I recovered my breath!

There was also the front office to man and radio control to be carried out. Nowadays the radio control is done centrally.

My court appearances as a cadet stood me in good stead, as I was soon involved in dealing with prisoners and attending court. My first Crown Court appearance was confusing as I had two different cases up for trial – and found myself being called for both at the same time!

Court attendance was something I grew to dislike intensely. I took no pleasure in having lawyers trying to rip my evidence to shreds or question my integrity – something I could not help but take personally, as I found it deeply offensive. It is little wonder that members of the public shy away from attending court, either as a victim of crime or a witness, afraid of a process that allows them to be treated so reprehensibly.

As an officer you soon discover that meeting new people is not always a pleasure – and naturally this can cut both ways. Police officers encounter the dregs of society on a frequent basis – where 'respect' and 'legal' are words never heard of, least of all ever practised.

I distinctly recall one occasion when I was sent to an address in Tring to issue a summons. The door was opened by a child of pre-school age who could barely reach the door handle. He took one look at me, then shouted out "Dad it's the f***ing pigs!" I stood there mouth agape with shock, in joyous anticipation of meeting the father, who snatched the summons from my hand with the grace of his child. As I looked again at the child I thought 'See you in a few years sonny' - after all he didn't stand a chance did he? With that the door was unceremoniously slammed in my face.

We did however, also meet some wonderfully spirited citizens, who, when the chips are down, can be relied upon to help their fellow man. It is all a balance of the good and bad – and no two days would ever be the same.

The first strip drugs search I carried out on a female was on a woman who just happened to be an old school friend - one of the hockey team no less! She had fallen into bad company and had become a heroin addict. She was being weaned off the drug with methadone. I was appalled to see what had once been a powerful body, full of vitality, now so emaciated. Unsure as to how she would react to me under these circumstances, I was grateful for her congeniality and we chatted freely. She told me she liked her new slender frame - God help her - but could shed no light as to how or why she found herself in this tragic position. The last I knew she was planning to move to Luton - I can only pray she managed to break her habit. To this day I don't know if she is alive or dead.

Police officers are rarely the purveyors of good news, unless of course a member of the public needs their help and is expecting their arrival. I always felt the police should have been given the role of informing people of their lottery win. Just for once it would have been great to make someone's day – instead of breaking it.

The delivery of so called 'agony messages' is a horrible job – which in the majority of instances was informing relatives that a loved one had died. This is something you can never get used to – it is not always known if the news is expected or not and you can never judge how the recipient will react.

One poor lady simply would not believe me when I had to tell her that her son had been killed, having crashed a vehicle that he'd stolen. She couldn't accept he would have stolen a car, therefore wouldn't believe he was dead!

Then there was a father, who, when informed his daughter had been murdered – had said to the officers "Why did you wake me up to tell me that?" He wasn't surprised and could not have cared less!

Probably the worse one I had to deliver was done in my probation. Together with the Sergeant we had to inform a man that his sixteen-year old son had died. He had left the road, inexplicably, on his motorbike and struck a lamppost – dying instantly. The father had bought the bike for his son's birthday and felt responsible for his death. It was such a cruel message to impart. His son, was a blond-haired youngster with the face of an angel and seeing the father's grief at the morgue was a levelling experience.

Death is just another hazard of the job, but no matter how removed you may become from the 'body' and what has happened to cause death, you can never walk away from the grieving family without a sense of the desolation you have left behind. It is an onerous task and one that enforces maturity beyond your own tender years.

In my probation I had to attend a post-mortem – this was a normal training exercise in those days. Having always had a fascination with human biology I wasn't phased by the experience. Certainly there were some macabre aspects to the process, but all in all I was intrigued. Even now I am fascinated with forensic science and pathology – but any thoughts of a career in that area end firmly with one word – 'decomposition'. While quite hardy, I know that I could not deal at such close quarters with some of the awful sights that befall the pathologist.

I realised I was already becoming hardened to the 'harsh realities of life' when I regaled the family with the tales of the mortuary over Sunday lunch and the fact that I had seen an old Sunday School teacher of mine 'in the fridge'. As mum's pallor took on a green hue I understood this was 'too much information'!

Many a time I had to force entry to houses to discover victims of sudden death – that became routine, but always you would attend with trepidation – and the ghoulish knowledge of what you will inevitably find. You would always pray the poor person would be asleep in bed or the armchair, and had only been there a day or two at most. I always remember handling my first corpse – which, as we were removing the clothes from its upper body, vomited its last supper all over me!

I was lucky – I never had badly decomposed bodies to handle – unlike one mate who found a body crawling with maggots – quite literally. I also managed to avoid suicides on the railway line – which, at Berkhamsted, was once not uncommon. I did have a few suicides at Ashridge to deal with – I recall one particular occasion when we had discovered a car with a pipe running from the exhaust into the vehicle. A man sat there with a photograph of his family beside him – such a sad scene. While attending this vehicle a man ran over to tell us there was another identical case in the trees one hundred yards away. At times of coping with death a 'sick sense' of humour kicks in – it has to, for self-preservation. It also helped that I strongly believe that the moment a person dies, they have moved on to a better place. The body, to me, is nothing but earthly remains – what made that person your 'loved one' and gave the body life was its spirit – the very thing that has moved on – and without it the body has no purpose. This makes it far easier to deal with a corpse 'physically' – it also helped me in coping when losing loved ones of my own.

I did, however, encounter a particularly tragic case of death by misadventure that had a very lasting impact on me. A man who had experimented with wearing articles of feminine attire accidentally hung himself from the shower rail in his bathroom. He left behind him a wife and two very young daughters.

The eldest child was a small toddler with a curly mop of 'orphan Annie' style hair. She had pronounced dimples, the most endearing smile and a marvellous line in incessant chatter – she was a real cherub.

On returning to the house a few days later to obtain a witness statement, the little girl suddenly looked at me, wide eyed and with a deep intake of breath she said "You must be

Jesus – you took my daddy away". What on earth do you say to that? I just looked at her mum, then back to the child, saying "My darling – if only I were!" Of course, she associated my presence with that of the undertakers who took her father's body away – and putting her Sunday school lessons into context with the event – thus I became Jesus. She broke my heart and received sweets from me for many months to come.

When you are dealing in the tragedies that befall others on a regular basis – witnessing the anguish and pain people are put through is a humbling experience. It puts into perspective what is really important in life. It also makes it harder to tolerate people who whinge incessantly about trivial inconveniences and those who fall out and argue with each other over nothing. Life is far too short to dwell on every drop of rain that falls into your life – there are always others worse off. It puts me in mind of that old adage; "I used to moan that I had no shoes, until I saw a man with no feet!"

Naturally, aside from the troubles and tragedies you encounter, there are many opportunities for fun and laughter. A wicked, and sometimes sick, sense of humour is tantamount to your survival. The banter in the canteen amongst colleagues was a lifeline. You knew if a colleague had just had a really grim job to deal with and how to pick them up and restore their spirits. There was ribbing here or there, or merciless teasing in some cases – but there was always the knowledge that the others understood how you felt, and from experience knew how to help you cope – to survive.

The 'powers that be' like to brandish banter these days as being 'canteen culture' laden only with racist comments and sexual innuendo unbecoming of the uniform. I can categorically say I never witnessed any racism amongst any of my colleagues - through my cadet-ship or eighteen years full service.

Yes, there were on occasions sexist remarks – but they weren't generally intended to offend, and after all, early on in my service, this was still very much a 'man's world'. If you couldn't accept some ribbing and teasing from your mates then you were in the wrong job –after all – certain quarters of the general public would dish out much worse than your colleagues ever could! As with every corner of society 'political correctness' has gone mad – to the detriment of normal human relationships and healthy interaction.

There are of course, numerous funny incidents and light moments in the police – after all when you are dealing with people, there's bound to be a few good laughs. The biggest laughs usually came through your own stupidity, or that of your colleagues. Like the time I was larking around with one of the guys and he lifted me off my feet – not clever when a lean, mean, police dog is in the office. The dog, 'Cash', promptly bit me on the bum, which everyone found hilarious apart from me – shall I just say it 'hurt'!

Then there was the time I attended the report of an intruder alarm at business premises in Tring. The Sergeant turned up close on my heels as 'back up'. He scaled an eight-foot high gate and I followed suit. I was wearing one of the old-style, totally impractical uniform skirts which restricted your movement to a large extent. On reaching the top of the gate I had to hoist my skirt up around my waist to negotiate the summit. As I sat with legs astride the gate the skipper decided to be gallant and turned to help me down. I was so embarrassed – but to his credit so was he!

Talking of being embarrassed, there was one occasion in High Street, Berkhamsted that lingers on in my memory for all time. I have a cousin, Alan, whom, if you knew him, you would describe as a big softie at heart. However, at that time – he was quite frightening in appearance. He was a heavily built guy, who wore hefty Doc Marten type boots, a long trench coat, and had a multi-coloured 'Mohican' style hair cut.

I was on foot patrol in the town centre, when Alan spotted me. He came bounding over, shouting 'Allo Cuz' and gave me a huge bear hug – lifting me clean off the ground as he did so. At this point, the Instant Response car – a marked police vehicle, was driving past. Seeing this tiny-framed, uniformed WPC being lifted from the deck by some hairy great Mohican was all they needed. With a massive screech of tyres and smoke issuing forth the car almost stood on its front wheels as it braked hard. Thankfully Alan put me back down and I got to the officers before they got to him – explaining rather sheepishly that we were cousins! I laugh about it now but I could have murdered Alan at the time.

The first ten years of my police service were spent in the front line. I worked across the entire Dacorum Division at Hemel Hempstead, Berkhamsted and Tring. Each station was different as were the respective towns. Hemel Hempstead, being the larger town was naturally busier generally with more public disorder situations. If you needed assistance you got a far quicker response due to the fact that there were a greater number of officers available.

Berkhamsted was a quiet town to work, although it had its moments of excitement and you would often work alone. Tring, being the smallest was surprisingly busy. At the time there were only two officers per shift there but it was common to find yourself running solo.

I attended numerous public order situations alone – but in truth found this quite effective. I recall one such incident at Tring Rugby club when a group of grown men were really 'getting stuck into each other'. As I walked up to them I must have been invisible. Tapping a huge guy on the shoulder, I said "Do you think you fellas might wrap this fight up and go home peacefully please?" He turned and looked down at me – all of 5'4", smiling sweetly with a hat perched on my head. Immediately he put his hands up, all contrite and apologetic and that was it – job done, they left without so much as a harsh word. Of course, that is a rare situation. You certainly wouldn't get away with that approach in Hemel Hempstead or with seventeen-eighteen year olds in Tring or Berkhamsted, but it worked for me many a time. Had a transit van full of male officers arrived on the scene the outcome may have been altogether different – more confrontational than a lone woman.

In smaller, more remote towns it is vital that you know how to talk to people and to play for time in dangerous moments. If you antagonise an already volatile situation you have a considerable wait until 'back up' arrives. In fact, in the outlying villages near Tring, Thames Valley Police were invariably the first to your rescue. It would be an education for officers from larger divisional stations to work in isolation now and again – that need for self-preservation changes your outlook and approach. Talking – communicating with people – that ultimately is the best tool you have. Of course using a few feminine wiles and a touch of coquettish flirting didn't go amiss either!

So what about specialisation within the police force? I certainly had no desire or interest in becoming a traffic officer. I enjoyed dealing with crime and criminals, but despite some of my closest friends being on the Criminal Investigation Department (CID) I didn't know if it would suit me permanently. In short I was undecided about what I really wanted to do, until by chance I fell into Intelligence work.

I was put on a four-week Home Office Large Major Enquiry System course (H.O.L.M.E.S) which is a computer system used to record the finer details of major crime investigations – such as rapes, murders, kidnaps etc.

My first job on H.O.L.M.E.S. was to finish up the remaining paperwork in connection with a murder. This was the murder of eighty-one year old Joan Macan from Ashridge in 1988 – a heinous crime against a former war heroine. It was to be the first of three occasions I would work on this enquiry, as well as having had operational input nearer the time of the offence. Much of the enquiry led the teams to members of the travelling fraternity and it was this factor that led me to develop a wide knowledge of these people which in turn led me to working on travelling criminals' intelligence.

I was involved with other major crime enquiries – the most notable being a kidnap situation. This was a highly charged, intense enquiry – with senior officers in charge knowing that their decisions could influence the outcome of the enquiry

– literally a matter of life or death. Thankfully after several days a milkman on his early rounds in Hemel Hempstead was alerted to sounds made by the kidnap victim who had been chained to the floor in a room over a shop.

The lady was rescued and excellent police work and surveillance brought the offender to justice. The lady and her family came into the incident room to see everyone who had been working on their behalf. It was a most rewarding moment – albeit extremely emotional and I don't mind admitting to the tears in my eyes. It is rare that those serving on inside Incident Room teams get to see those for whom they are working. It was a delight, not to mention sheer relief, to see the lady safe and well - a very brave woman indeed.

Following on from the Joan Macan murder enquiry, computerised travelling criminals intelligence was set up in Hertfordshire. I was fortunate enough to be in the right place at the right time and so found my niche in this arena, in the process becoming the best of friends with Rosie Lenthall (now Metcalf, who has since emigrated to America).

I spent some seven years working on this intelligence and was proud that Hertfordshire led the way in the Home Counties in this field. We had a small group of outside field officers who gleaned fantastic information and two of us on the inside helping make connections. My most personally rewarding moment was when an officer at Harpenden phoned to make an enquiry. He was dealing with a rape allegation and had a registration number of a suspect vehicle seen in the area. Although the number was incorrect in two areas my in-depth knowledge of the intelligence meant I could identify straight away who the owner was.

I contacted the officers in the field, who did a fabulous job with the arrest and interview of the offender, who ultimately received nine years imprisonment for his trouble. He was also a main protagonist involved in a series of club and pub breaks we had been investigating. The offenders would 'ram raid' their way into clubs or pubs stealing the contents, and in many cases the entire fruit machine from within – this particular modus operandi ceased upon their arrest and remained obsolete for several years to come.

Of course, computer systems are only as good as the data loaded onto them. I was lucky to have a retentive mind – what I entered onto the computer stayed in my head too, so I could always supply a fair answer to anyone's enquiries if the computer was out of action. Intelligence work suited me – I had an aptitude for it and got a real buzz from making connections between crime and suspects. I assisted more officers with information leading to the arrests of offenders than I could ever have hoped to achieve on the beat or even on CID. I revelled in it and it made me tick.

When the murder of Joan Macan was reopened again in 1994, I was glad to be involved. I was part of a small team of officers who created a fantastic working atmosphere. They worked hard, played hard and above all, wanted one thing only – to get the offenders convicted for this despicable murder.

The team wanted it almost as much for the Senior Investigating Officer in Charge (S.I.O) – Dick Pottinger, for whom this case was (and always remained) a sticker - that being a term generally meaning a case in which you know who the offenders are, but have insufficient evidence to secure a conviction.

Working on such a serious crime, with wonderful colleagues makes you appreciate truly what 'camaraderie' is all about. You get to know everyone's little foibles – strengths, weaknesses – the lot! You have complete trust in one another, you can laugh together and cry together. Times like these are where lasting friendships are formed – and in my case, some time later, when love jumped up and bit me at a time I least expected it to.

So – what of the enquiry itself – did we get justice? To our enduring desolation the answer is "No". Sadly the Crown Prosecution Service lacked the commitment that was held by our team and offered no evidence instead of pursuing the true path of justice - which was capable of being achieved. The entire team was devastated. Each one of us had given every ounce of our being to the enquiry not to mention hours in unpaid time – from the S.I.O. down. It is hard, so hard, when you know who has committed a crime but you simply cannot secure a conviction. We just pray that Joan Macan knows we did everything we possibly could.

Some months later, Steve Wheatley and I identified the body of one of the main suspects in this offence, after he had died of a heart attack. The other main suspect remains incarcerated in a high-security unit, having been convicted of other offences of extreme violence to innocent members of the public. I sincerely hope he never comes out, as he will always pose a serious danger to others and blood would surely spill.

I continued working on 'travelling criminals' intelligence in the Force Intelligence Bureau until 1997 when I went to Hatfield as the Local Intelligence Officer. It was good to have a change of emphasis and I enjoyed working on all areas of intelligence work. Hatfield wasn't the ideal base for me as I had very little local knowledge – although very soon acquired it. I was delighted when the position of Local Intelligence Officer became vacant in Dacorum, at Hemel Hempstead facilitating a sideways move for me - it was like coming home after many years absent.

Dacorum was special to me – so many really good friends around me, a great working environment and of course, the benefit of local knowledge. I had a fabulous five months there before leaving the police in May 1998. My reasons for leaving are clear later – suffice to say my partner was retiring after thirty-one years service and I chose to leave with him as I still had twelve years service to run – far too long to subject him to!

There are many people who are indelibly etched in my mind for one reason or another – too numerous of course to mention – but most of whom I worked with at various times, or worked for. Sandy Murray for one – nicknamed the 'screaming skull' made me shudder as a probationer.

Sandy was a brash Glaswegian who was infamous for ordering a baton charge amid public disorder in Queen's

Square, Hemel Hempstead. He was not a man to be crossed, nor the Inspector to be on duty when you 'got it wrong'. I found this out to my cost one night and learned the error of my ways in 'double quick time'. Like most probationers, I gave him a wide berth - but came to respect him as he got the best out officers.

Lesley is another with whom much of my social time in the early police years was spent. We had been cadets together, and when she was posted as a WPC to Berkhamsted, naturally we became very close – in fact we were inseparable and known collectively as 'Tweedle Dum' and 'Tweedle Dee'. We have drifted apart over the years but I will always remember the fantastic times we had together, the deep friendship and understanding we shared.

One man who I always feel indebted to, is Jeff Thompson. At a time when we had a major crisis in our family, Jeff came to my rescue. He gave me endless support, which in turn enabled me to give of my best to my family. I can never repay him adequately for taking such a huge weight off my shoulders.

I will always remember with affection, tinged with great sadness, three officers in Dacorum, who died whilst I served there. Dave Pearce tragically died, aged forty years, just over a year after having a heart transplant. Frank Mason, twenty-seven years – was shot at point blank range while off duty and trying to intervene in a bank robbery at Hemel Hempstead; and Stuart Marvin who died of lung cancer aged thirty-five years. They were lovely people and each one was far too young to die. May they rest peacefully and know they touched so many lives and hearts along the way, no matter how short the path. Police funerals are invariably deeply emotive. For anyone killed in the course of duty there is always that 'it could have been me' scenario buzzing around inside your head, but more importantly, there is a kindred spirit – they are part of your other, much larger family.

I have never had any regrets about my chosen career. There were times I hated 'the job', times I loved it, but overall, it was the best grounding in life I could ever have had. However, as one who has been in 'Civvy Street' now for over nine years, I can see a certain insular nature to the police force.

I see many retired officers going back to civilian roles within the police, but am glad I didn't do this. There are great people outside the job too – it might not be such a close-knit club, but good people all the same – with the odd one or two who understand and share the same wicked sense of humour! I do miss intelligence work – the buzz – the connections and the chase but am glad to be able to work for myself and do something different.

There is still a yearning within me for what I call a 'real job' – by that I mean one in which I am 'helping society'. I think I have a public service ethic within me, which will never go. I have the same values now as before and a true sense of justice. I firmly feel that although you can take yourself out of the 'force' you can never completely take the 'force' out of you.

In tandem with 'growing up' in the world of police work, I had also matured considerably on a personal level. I bought my first house as a twenty-one year old - a little terraced 'turn of the century' cottage on Northchurch High Street. I had been putting things aside for my 'bottom drawer' for a couple of years - soon after my first big expense of a motor car.

The day I moved out of home was hard on both mum and me - we both cried - she, for the fact that her fledgling had finally flown the nest, and me, feeling guilty for making her feel so sad.

Once I was settled, mum regularly popped in for lunch or cups of tea - and we formed a different, more adult relationship where the playing field was now level and an understanding far deeper.

The house was a total mess when I bought it - the previous owners' dog was smelly and the carpets needed so much 'Shake 'n' Vac' it almost made them crusty - until I had redecorated and could rip them up. The first house you buy is probably the one into which you pour the most energy. I was proud of my little house and loved making it a home, piece by piece.

I soon learned the art of financial management and budgeting, diligently recording my outgoings so that I knew what was spare or spoken for. With the exception of my mortgage, I had nothing on hire purchase - dad had certainly instilled good financial values in me. If I couldn't afford it I didn't have it. I didn't make use of dad's decorating skills unless I really couldn't manage something myself - like the incredibly steep stairwell. I can still see dad on his steps and boards with the agility of a ballerina dancing his way from one end to the other on the high rise of the stairs. He was a far braver man than I.

I stayed in my cottage for five years before moving to a larger house which, ironically backed onto the cottage. It was a modern house with a mono-pitched roof and although I was happy there, it never captured my affections quite like my first home. The interest rates went up to fifteen per-cent just after this move, and with money all spent it was at least six months later before I could cover the bathroom floor and carpet the lounge.

Five years later, just after the housing market collapsed I moved in 1993 to Welwyn Garden City and a pretty cottage, although, unlike my first property, this one was modern. The move wasn't simple - I was initially chain of seven people, and the person at the bottom was unable to get a mortgage so it collapsed. Six months, one week later we were back in business. As the survey on the cottage had expired by one week I had to pay the same building society to carry out the same survey on the same house. It was a painful experience this move, but another education none the less.

Living on my own gave me tremendous self-confidence and made my already independent streak more fiercely so. I tried my hand at anything and everything rather than asking for help. Most things I found achievable to some extent and it gave me great satisfaction.

Holidaying alone was something else I was not afraid of. I dipped my toe into the water gently to start with on a seven-day trip to Majorca. It felt like everyone at the airport was staring at me and even worse when I got off the transfer coach - the only one staying at my particular hotel. I soon felt more comfortable about it, later taking ten days and then two weeks on my own - after all it was no different to living alone - just better, as I had no chores or work to think about.

In those days I just lay prostrate on beaches all day - not something I do now. I never came home without a deep tan and always felt refreshed. People were far friendlier to me as a single traveller, than they are to couples or groups. Middle-aged folk latched onto me with ease and were really good company - it was me, the youngster that cried off early needing sleep, before they ever did!

If you are thinking I am a loner, then you are mistaken - but I am comfortable with my own company. I never get bored and am happy to take all that life throws at me. Living and holidaying alone were just part of my personal development, although of course, it is far nicer to have someone to share things with. I'd be a liar if I said I never got lonely - I did and sometimes it felt as if the walls were closing in on me, but generally I was fine. Enhanced by life in the police force the path to maturity was being well pounded.

CHAPTER 6

THE GREEN, GREEN GRASS OF HOME

As a Northchurch ex-pat, so to speak, I miss the familiar environment of my youth. I particularly miss the common and canal walks. I suppose from the age of sixteen in 1978 through to 1993 I had a few occasions when I was not living in Northchurch, however it wasn't until 1993 that I moved away from the area with any degree of permanency, to Welwyn Garden City. Alas, I haven't lived in Northchurch since then.

Of course with my family still living in the village I was, and am, a frequent visitor back home. Before dad died, he, mum and I would get out walking as much as we could - I hungered to see my homeland. I still love nothing better, time permitting, than to get out over the common with mum. There is actually no such place as Northchurch Common – despite local use of the name and its appearance on maps. It is all part of Berkhamsted Common and lies adjacent to the beautiful Ashridge Forest with its maze of interlinking paths. The area known as 'Northchurch Common' stretches west from the top of the B4506, New Road, Northchurch to the top end of the sleepy hamlet of Dudswell.

There is a plethora of flora and fauna if you are prepared to look for it and this area is largely untapped, save for a few locals and dog walkers. While it is a great place to walk a dog this does have the disadvantage of disturbing the colonies of deer sheltering within.

There is a typical walk that I have taken on many occasions. I have been out there in every season and at varying times of the day. I have never yet been disappointed – always seeing something different. It is just a wonderful place to be. I thought I might share my observations on one such walk with you.

"Spring was turning into early summer as I strolled over the common exploring every nook and cranny of the familiar territory.

In early March before spring took a firm hold, the bracken had been in its brown winter state of stubble and the trees bare - but the pervading air of peace, as always, endured.

Today, like another world, in a new season, the common is resplendent, cloaked in every shade of green. The low bracken fronds are starting to unfurl, stems gaining height with every kiss of the sun and sway of the breeze.

Bird song in the spring warmth - from crows to blackbirds, magpies, tits and sparrows, is deafening. Squirrels hop in silent staccato movements - tails dancing in their wake, while the rustle and crackle of leaves gives away those foraging in the dry scrub. I inhale deeply the rich, earthy smell, offset by the freshness of new bracken - my panacea to cure all ills.

Then I hear it, loud and clear - the song of the cuckoo - and it just keeps singing.

Walking into deeper shade I catch sight of the commons' best kept secret - its deer - seated under the trees to the left, ears silhouetted in the darkness. My eyes are well trained to spot them. I move quietly on, not wishing to disturb their rest, knowing I am subjected to their watchful vigil. Catching a movement to my right I am rewarded with more deer moving away from the walkways and rides. Dog walkers over yonder have hastened them along. Even if you don't see them, fresh deer and rabbit droppings along the way betray their presence.

Reaching the top of the common the land opens out at the mercy of the elements with its wispy grass, dancing gracefully in the wind. The yellow gorse flowers have faded, heralding summers' arrival. Blue speedwell and buttercups abound, - pink cranesbill and yellow lamium randomly grace the paths. Butterflies flit about amidst the frantic activity of the birds. The dawn chorus here must be a truly splendid orchestra!

At the spinney to my north the treasure trove bursts open again as an entire colony of deer emerges. There is a mix of young and mature, pale and dark - no signs of any stags – they are seldom seen this far south, only on an early morning ride along the highway or deeper into Ashridge forest. The colony is untroubled by my observation… and still the cuckoo sings. I am reminded of a charming verse about the cuckoo, which my mother once recited from her youth:

> 'In April I open my bill
> In May I sing night and day,
> In June I change my tune,
> In July away I fly,
> In August, away I must'.

Moving into the deep hollow at the summit, the grassy rides become narrower and stony. The ground is hard and dry - I can scarcely believe it is still just May. Dog roses scramble up trees, their pink flowers hanging like a garland. The vista opens up across the valley, the town laid out before me, nestled amidst emerald green fields and framed by trees.

The trappings of the world continue: the faint sounds of distant traffic; a train's rattle echoes up the valley; an aeroplane overhead - all are silenced by the birds.

This was my adolescent playground, a place for contemplation, teenage problem solving, or to simply 'be'. Rabbits used to literally hop around me then - not so today.

From the common I pass into the top of Norcott Hill, leaving cuckoo song fading in my wake. I pause at a barred gate to a field, where I used to stroke resident horses, and watch deer or rabbits. The long grass keeps its inhabitants a firm secret today.

At the bottom of the hill, in Dudswell, I stand a while on the canal bridge - a pretty spot, with a lock cottage that was once a sweetshop and, prior to that, a pub. To extend my walk I take the towpath along the Grand Union Canal back to New Road. The resident herons are commonly seen in majestic pose on the canal banks - so statuesque that you could easily miss them if they didn't move.

A family of ducklings paddles over to chirp greetings, praying bread is on offer - alas I have none! Growing fast with mounting independence, the remaining fluffy feathers belie their tender age. A female coot on her nest shields two offspring, not yet ready to leave the safety of her wing. Unsteadily they make comical attempts to stand.

A flash of blue catches my eye - there she goes, that most beautiful of birds - the kingfisher. So fast is its movement I am grateful for the sunlight, which illuminated its turquoise wings - what a joy to behold! Further along the towpath rabbits skit on the far bank – the railway sidings are their home, where they are untroubled by man. I regard it as my own 'Watership Down'.

An adult moorhen next appears followed by three of its tiny young, so small, black and fluffy. Bobbing along behind they skim the water in vain attempt to keep up with the pace.

Previously I have seen foxes following the edge of the railway track - not so on this venture. Maybe 'Mother Nature' feels I've had quite enough for one day - a walk full of riches.

Whatever the hour or season there are bountiful treasures to uncover. I implore you to remove the blindfold, stop and stare - it's all there to see if you take the time to look! It's a busy place, the countryside."

So this is 'home' – in the context of my roots, my family, my childhood and much of my adult life. 'As the saying goes "Home is where the heart is" – therefore I was blessed with two homes – the one I shared with my beloved husband – and Northchurch.

I recently had the utter privilege of spending a few hours with Bert Hosier, famous locally as 'Hedgehog', for an article I was writing.

Bert has written articles for Northchurch St Mary Church newsletter for some thirty-two years and published a book in 1994 – "Hedgehog's Northchurch". The book is part of my heritage - the life and times of so many characters have been fundamental in shaping those of my own grandparents and parents with three generations of my family attending the village school.

Bert's use of language, especially local dialect is colourful, leaving the reader in no doubt as to pronunciation and interpretation. It provides humour, tragedy and above all leaves you with a sense of knowing where you come from.

When I asked Bert how he would sum up the Northchurch of today, with that of his youth, he replied "Greatly enlarged, and full of strangers". He is so right - even I can see there have been numerous changes in the village since my youth - and not all for the better.

One innovation that looks great is the new village sign – its presence having been instigated by Bert. It lends some pictorial character to the grass verge between the High Street and the parade of shops.

Another person who has always played a pivotal role in the village, being involved in most everything that goes on – is Councillor Alan Fantham. Alan might not be everyone's favourite villager as he is very forthright in his opinions. He may not always make popular decisions, but what he most certainly does – is care with a passion about the village and works incredibly hard on its behalf.

It is easy to criticise others from your armchair – it is quite another to put yourself on offer. I admire Alan's tenacity and dedication and feel the village owes him a great debt.

It wasn't until I moved away from Northchurch that I *truly* appreciated what a major part of my life it is. Maybe one day I will return – who knows, but for sure I will always be back visiting in some capacity or another. I will undoubtedly get the same feeling as I do now, when I come down Darrs Lane, with the common opening up before me on the other side of the valley. Being in another place and time does not diminish the homeland of the first thirty-two years of my life. It will always hold a special place in my heart.

Somewhere Over the Rainbow

Northchurch Common - summer    Northchurch Common - autumn

Dudswell lock and cottages    Northchurch St Mary's

Northchurch sign    Church & School from New Road canal bridge

CHAPTER 7

CHASING RAINBOWS

Love is an enigma
With no defining rules,
For family and friends
Or old romantic fools.

It can lift you or destroy you,
Make you whole or torn apart,
Love is an emotion
Not for the faint in heart.

It often requires sacrifice
And frequently gives pain,
But the bounty of the harvest
Thrives on sun and rain.

The rough and smooth go hand in hand,
With compromise the key,
So sad that many folk are blind
And simply will not see...

That love just isn't easy,
Nothing cut and dried,
But when it comes, receive it
With arms held open wide.

For my entire life – or so it seemed, on a personal level I was *'Chasing Rainbows'* – searching for that elusive pot of gold. For me that was 'love, romance, *Mr. Right*, marriage and children'.

If I cast my mind back I should have known the path of true love was never going to run smooth for me. As I gave my collected pocket money of three weeks (a total of 15d) to Simon, aged somewhere between six and nine years old – I failed to notice he only had eyes for my best friend Lynda at the time. Well, you couldn't blame him – I swear she was gorgeous from birth – not a knee-scraping tomboy like me. It didn't matter though – it still hurt to feel rejected. One boy in the class, Steven, did take a shine to me and gave me a ring – but of course, he wasn't the one for me, so, like most children, I recall saying something hurtful to him!

Then at Middle School – I fell for the ginger-haired Michael, who had the voice of a choirboy before it broke. I remember hearing him sing at a joint schools concert – before I met him – his voice was amazing. He referred to me as 'Two Ton Tessie' as I suffered with puppy fat between the ages of ten and thirteen in particular.

I did get to go on a date with another 'Michael' when I was twelve – but didn't like the sloppy kiss he gave me, so I 'chucked him', as the expression goes, the next day – having had no breakfast as I was so worried about telling him.

At Senior School – Ashlyns, first I was in love with Neil, known as 'Stan' and had his name tattooed in felt tip across the back of my hand. Alas, one lunchtime the classroom fell silent as they watched Stan and Alison engaged in a good old 'snog'. Time to give up - I couldn't compete with that!

Then came the biggest love of my school life – the one that really broke my heart – Tony Miles. I was fourteen years old. We were in the library when we accidentally brushed hands whilst clamouring for books. It was like getting an electric shock – there was a surge of heat emanating from his hand that attracted me like a magnet. Tony was fairly short and stocky, enjoyed tennis and football – and like me, was an avid Liverpool Football Club supporter.

I was besotted – we did actually become friends although how conversation ever started I really don't know. I guess one of my friends must have started the ball rolling with the 'my friend fancies you' sort of intro! Anyway – I did get to chat with Tony when he came into school of a morning – fortuitously he used the entrance right by my classroom, so I would loiter on the radiator in excited anticipation of his arrival. We always spoke about the latest Liverpool match if nothing else. At lunchtime I would hope he was playing tennis so I could sit with my tape recorder nearby with my friends.

I liked the music of Genesis – fuelled further by the fact that Tony did as well, so I played it for his benefit. If Tony wasn't there, I would sit on the glorious fields at Ashlyns or play tennis myself and hope he would pass by on his travels.

I would occasionally walk home with Tony after school, if I didn't have hockey practice. Well, what I really mean, is I would make a point of locating him on the walk home and scurry hell for leather to catch up with him, or dawdle so he caught me up! No doubt I would have chatted inanely away – funny but I don't really recall much of the chat at all.

I remember well the day that tore my fragile adolescent heart apart. There was Tony – in the corridor by my classroom – my heart leapt. Then I stalled as I saw him in conversation with my best friend, Karen. Both of them seemed to ignore me. A few minutes later she told me he had asked her out. I couldn't speak – I hurt so much. I managed, at least, to wait until Karen went off to her next lesson before allowing my guttural sobs to spill over. Why did I always have friends seemingly more attractive to the opposite sex than me - why was I still too much of a tomboy, without the womanly curves of my friends, or their coquettish charms? I've asked myself those questions a million times over – and now laugh at the thought. I am 'me' – take it or leave it – alas – all too often my heart's desire chose to leave it!

Of course, what made it worse is that Karen had no interest in Tony whatsoever. It became a painful issue for me throughout the rest of my school days. I did go to a party to which Tony had also been invited. I actually got to have a kiss and cuddle from him – very generous of him, but no, I was 'a girl next door type' – not for him. This was probably evidenced by the fact that he asked me if I wanted to go to watch Liverpool FC play at Queens Park Rangers with him and his mate – did I ever? Wow – having followed Liverpool since the age of nine years old this was the first chance I had had to see them play. The Reds won the match and I enjoyed the goal twice as much as anyone else - I was there with Tony, who gave me a big hug as we leapt up and down when the ball rattled the back of the net. Bliss!

Tony was really chuffed for me when I was accepted into the Police cadets. He actually wrote to me a couple of times during my first year as a cadet - I was quite thrilled about it.

As with all things, time waits for no man. My life had taken off in a new direction and although I bumped into Tony a couple of times in town during the next five years I haven't seen him now for some twenty-plus years. I know he got his PhD and was in the London area afterwards. I still think about him occasionally and wonder how his life turned out. I'd love to bump into him, share a coffee and swap notes on how our lives have evolved.

The unrequited love in my life did not stop on leaving school. Aged sixteen, going on seventeen years, when I joined the police cadets I was at that age when relationships form strongly in your mind. I still wore rose-coloured glasses – not just in terms of 'life experience' but also where 'love and romance' were concerned.

I guess my beau in the cadets was Lee – a person I didn't like at all initially – he seemed cocky and arrogant. In the end it turned out he was a real sweetie, great fun with a lovely warm smile. Lee liked me too, I know, but not quite enough – guess I was just a buddy at the end of the day.

As the big, bad world beckoned me forward I was looking forward to my police career, but still pined for love, marriage and to have children.

I made a complete hash of most relationships – it seemed the moment someone became important to me, so they vanished into thin air. I obviously sent out scary signals to the opposite sex – although I never advertised my dreams of settling down and having a family. I think I just tried too hard most of the time.

I also discovered the perils of 'married men'. As a naïve eighteen-year old I had little awareness of how easily I could be manipulated. As a result I made myself incredibly unhappy at times through my own foolish decisions and choices.

While others castigate people who get involved in such relationships, I know how easy it is for someone craving romantic affection to be drawn into such situations and therefore I have sympathy for those involved. I think I had a notice on my forehead that read "Prize mug - just tell me you love me and I'll believe it".

Having experienced bad relationships it made me appreciate the good ones all the more. I enjoyed great friendship with several men throughout my police career – being in a 'man's world' meant you often ended up with a higher proportion of male friends than female. I feel that men make fantastic friends – they are far less judgemental than women and give honest appraisals of given situations and candid advice.

I felt like I was always 'in love' with someone or other – I had idols in both the celebrity world and real life. My ideological concept of being 'in love' caused me no end of heartache, but I guess it is all part of growing up! You might think I have many regrets – in truth I don't, as life has many harsh lessons to serve up – and I learned the hard way.

I was so lonely, 'romantically', at one point that I decided to join a 'singles club' - an early form of dating agency, I guess - but I bottled out of a first 'date'. I lost my nerve completely and cried off. Despite my confidence in most areas of life I had none when it came to the male of the species.

Somewhere Over the Rainbow

I almost became engaged to a fireman, Jimmy, that I went out with for a time and have great memories, in particular of his parents, Dennis and Esther. Dennis and 'Essie' are adorable people – Irish, passionate and so very kind. They remain very dear to my heart and we still exchange Christmas cards some twenty-five years later.

I did become engaged when I was twenty-five – to my brother's friend, Ian. We had been through a highly traumatic experience as a family (see 'He Ain't Heavy' – Chapter 8) and Ian had been incredibly supportive. As a child I had always had a soft spot for Ian, which was rekindled during this period. We had been friends all our lives, but were drawn closer together by the trauma and a few months later became 'an item', as they say. Of course, when you are in given stressful situations emotions run high - a result of which led me to misinterpret my love for a friend as 'romantic love'. I noticed pretty soon that we were starting to bicker and make each other unhappy. Having got engaged at Christmas 1986 I caused a major upset by breaking it off six weeks or so later. Naturally, it initially caused strife amongst our families, but it was an honest decision and the correct call to make. Ian and I both wanted similar things from life – it would have been easy to let things progress. I firmly believe that if you cannot be true unto yourself then you can never be true to others. I could not go ahead with what would have amounted to living a lie.

I cared deeply for Ian and I felt tremendous guilt in hurting him. I am delighted that he is now happily married with two children – yes, it assuages my guilt – but more than that – it reaffirms that I made the right decision.

I have several friends – all between their late thirties and forties who have recently thrown their corsets into the dating arena. With the working lives of so many men and women being hectic, there is no easy way to meet a potential lifelong partner or companion. Having various options available to you one could be fooled into thinking it would be a breeze

– not so it seems! On the plus side at least there is no longer a stigma attached to the whole process.

My friends have asked me if I think it is 'safe' to go to an agency, or to look on dating websites - having heard about the perils of chat rooms, dates gone 'horribly wrong' or youngsters being led astray by people old enough to know better. My view is that 'it' can be no more dangerous than meeting people at nightclubs or pubs. There you have to keep one hand on your handbag and the other firmly on your drink to ensure you are neither robbed of your valuables or of anything far more precious via drugs being slipped into the slim-line tonic you thought you'd ordered.

So how do you stake your claim in the dating world? Firstly you need to prepare something akin to a personal Curriculum Vitae of your life. Sounds simple – but getting the correct balance might be tricky. You have to make yourself sound desirable without portraying yourself as the queen of the catwalk (unless of course, you are). You need to be interesting or fun, kind and thoughtful - stating your case without misleading the potential date.

How picky you can afford to be is another dilemma. Set your stakes too high in the mate you are seeking, and you're bound to be left out in the cold. Desire a partner with nothing less than a Masters degree or Rolls Royce and you're sure to be disappointed. One particular friend did exactly this – reasoning that she wanted someone extremely intelligent with which to engage in stimulating conversation and improve her vocabulary. There is nothing wrong with setting high standards – if, of course there's any choice out there - but the danger with pigeon-holing people is that you narrow the field immensely. Who's to say you aren't missing out on an amazingly interesting, clever companion, who simply had no chance or desire to go to university.

Another friend has been sent countless mismatches from her agency. The first one has been immortalised as the 'comb over man'. She is mortified to think that in order to meet her date she turned down dinner with my husband and me.

So as we tucked into our roast beef, she sat in a mutually agreed pub, carnation wilting under the incessant chat of a man who sported a mere couple of strands of hair - deftly combed across his balding pate in vintage 'Ralph Coates' style. Quite apart from the fact he spoke only of himself all night and bored her to tears, she simply couldn't get past his head to take him seriously. The next fella was better in the conversational department but tragically had no front teeth. This immediately put my friend off, with the thought of tongue wrestling relegated to well beyond the dentist's chair. Thirdly came a man who, while not too much older than she, had aged well before his time. To his credit he was very gentlemanly and courteous, but alas, he was more 'Zimmer' than zip - no basis upon which to want to meet again.

As my friend bemoans – "I don't ask much - just for someone to have a head of their own hair, a full set of teeth, and enough power in his legs to stand unaided". I wait with baited breath to hear the next instalment!

Having checked out a few dating websites for friends, I have to say I was quite impressed - it's like having your very own *'male order'* catalogue! You get a sneak preview physically (well, the face at least) even if you can't be sure what they write about themselves is totally kosher. You don't even have to leave the comfort of home to have a browse.

So if you fancy a bit of 'window shopping' for men online isn't a bad option. Personally speaking, agencies or online would never be an option for me - I know I haven't the bottle!

My own quest for love continued on a fruitless path during the following years (well almost a decade to be precise). A pattern of good man, bad man relationships ensued, until the light at the end of the tunnel finally beckoned – enter Dick, my darling husband and soul mate – he was so worth the wait and any amount of heartache. (See 'The Pot of Gold' – Chapter 11).

For me, the moral of the story of 'Chasing rainbows' is never to close your heart to others, but to forget chasing that which is out of reach – live, enjoy and let it happen naturally.

CHAPTER 8

HE AIN'T HEAVY

*'You'll never walk alone' is our anthem,
It conveys all one could say,
And big brother you are surely my hero,
For your will always finds a way.*

We think it's cancer" the ward sister told me as I sat in her office. Deep down I had guessed, but really didn't want to hear it - the lump in my throat threatened to strangle me, my stomach knotted tightly.

My brother, Martin is now a handsome, tanned and fit man of forty-eight years. To watch him out running or at work on the grounds of the Collegiate School, Berkhamsted, you simply wouldn't imagine the traumas that have beset him during the past twenty-two years. There are tell-tale signs if you look at the scars on his chest and abdomen, but what you'll see most is a man that enjoys life to the full - and how he has earned that right!

As kids, he and I were pretty close. I followed him around like a sheep. We would play football and cricket and race up and down the road. Broken windows and vases abounded as we ran amok.

We fought like cat and dog and I am ashamed to say I would resort to 'biting' if all else failed. Martin played rough and I learned early on that you had to stand tall and fight back. He was my favourite companion and I sought his approval every inch of the way.

Even as his 'kid sister' I would have protected Martin against anything or anyone bad if it were at all possible. In those days he lacked my confidence, but made up for that with sheer effort in everything he did. His industrious nature was to stand him in good stead just when he needed it most.

Over a period of a few short months early in 1985 Martin started suffering back pain. Never one to be sick, he went to the doctors - the first of several trips to no avail. He then started to have stomach pain, so bad he couldn't eat. This was a sure sign that all was not right, as Martin has one of the most voracious appetites for food that I know. He lost two stone in the space of six weeks, and finally a doctor said she would refer him to a specialist. He had been prescribed painkillers, then sleeping tablets, but nothing helped. Martin was surviving on these and orange juice, until one morning at work he could continue no longer and had to go home. His fiancée, Julie (now his wife) called a doctor out and wouldn't take 'no' for an answer - he needed to go to hospital. It was Friday 7th June 1985.

At West Herts Hospital, Hemel Hempstead he was seen by Mr Nicholls. It was on visiting Martin that I had spoken to the sister in her office. I was told he would need to go to Charing Cross hospital, London but that would be early the next week. I spent the entire weekend in deep torment. I couldn't tell Julie, or mum and dad, as the diagnosis hadn't been confirmed yet - what if it wasn't cancer? Please God, let it not be cancer! Martin was twenty-six years old - far too young to die.

On Monday 10th June I received a call from the hospital, saying they couldn't get an ambulance for Martin's transfer to Charing Cross - could I take him? Otherwise he'd have to wait a few days. No option there, I thought. Julie and I went to the hospital to collect him, London A-Z to hand. The sister saw us first and confirmed they were sure he had cancer. Poor Julie's sharp intake of breath was palpable, such was her shock. I wished I had confided in her to soften the inevitable blow.

On arrival at Charing Cross, he was placed under the consultancy of Mr Ed Newlands, who later became a Professor, and has subsequently tragically died early into his retirement.

He was a friend of Mr Nicholls and an expert in the field of cancer. He immediately carried out a biopsy.

Julie and I went shopping for pyjamas and dressing gown for Martin on our return home - we were in a state of numb shock - it was surreal.

The next onerous job task was telling my parents. As a police officer at the time, I had delivered many agony messages, but none such as this one - it was the worse one ever.

Later that evening, Martin phoned to confirm that he had testicular cancer. It was bad, naturally, but curable. Hell - deep hell, where would all this take us? Mr Newlands gave no odds of survival, no figures - just hope - a mighty fine thing too, as the odds would have been alarmingly bad. Martin had a teratoma, which was particularly aggressive and fast moving.

So advanced was the cancer that it had moved out of the testicles, he had a four-inch tumour on the stomach; he had it in his liver (which was twice its normal size), the chest and neck. As the primary source of the cancer couldn't be identified, the 'unknown' offending testicle could not be removed - a factor which became significant much later on.

The subject of using a sperm bank arose before chemotherapy (chemo) was administered, as chemo would eradicate any existing sperm in the system. Both he and Julie declined this, just wanting to get on with treating the disease. In hindsight, they would now urge anyone else take the opportunity that they declined.

Chemo started right away. We visited him next day, with mum feeling she wouldn't be able to face him without dissolving into tears. Of course, once she saw him, she was fine - and brave for her only son whose life was being imperilled by this dreadful disease.

The first course was soon over and he was to have a ten-day rest to allow his blood cells time to recover before the next treatment. This is essential as the chemo wipes out healthy cells as well as 'bad' ones and the body needs to rebuild the defences before it can withstand more chemo.

During the respite period Martin got worse - much worse. He lost even more weight and looked positively skeletal. It was tough too on Julie, as Martin wouldn't let her near him physically or emotionally. He knew he was a bag of bones, and simply felt so ill. He spent much time in bed and was sick with most anything he tried to eat or drink.

I will never forget taking him back to Charing Cross for his next treatment. Julie and I were terrified. He could barely walk up the escalator and we had to get a wheelchair to take him any further. At that time we didn't realise it, but the chemo had resulted in his duodenum swelling - so much, that not even fluid could pass through, thus he had become seriously dehydrated. Martin was whisked into the ward and placed on an 'emergency' drip. It was so very hard to leave the hospital that day.

With great trepidation, the following day, Julie, Ian and I, visited. Our sighs of relief were almost tangible as we saw a chirpy, round-faced and rosy-cheeked Martin. He looked like a different person altogether, fabulous, and it was with lighter hearts that we came away that evening.

We came to realise that Martin was the one who kept us going throughout this awful time - if he was up, so were we. If he had a bad day, so did we! As family or friend you can only 'be there' for love, support and practical assistance. In truth that is all you can do for anyone with serious illness - you are on the periphery. The rest is out of your control - a private battle between patient, illness and the medical profession.

The next three weeks were gruelling for us all. Martin remained in hospital on drip feeds and chemo, and was 'nil by mouth'. There was obviously great consternation amongst Mr Newlands and his team, and talk of an emergency operation. Before the operation was to become a reality, they did their final scans in preparation - and some kind of miracle started to happen. There were signs that the tumour on the stomach was starting to shrink - the chemo had at long last kicked in, and the operation never took place.

Our daily routine continued and gradually Martin was able to eat again. We took him any food we could get our hands on as, while the medical care was superb, the hospital food was dire. It was a wonderful day when we could bring him home again for a respite period between treatments. Julie and I went down early one Saturday morning to collect him. Usually the journey would take up to two hours - having the M25 and A40 traffic to contend with. This morning it took forty-five minutes and he was still eating breakfast when we arrived.

Chemo continued for the following ten months and we settled into a pattern of visits, collecting and returning Martin to and from the hospital. A Hickman line was installed into his chest to save him from the painful practice of repeatedly having needles inserted into his arms. The line meant that the drugs went straight into his main arteries, and could be capped for when he was at home.

We made a mistake on one occasion, when Martin told me not to stay while he was awaiting readmission. It was then found that his white blood cell count (and therefore his immunity) was too low to enable the next course of chemo to go ahead. He had to phone Julie to collect him as I'd already left - and didn't have a mobile phone in those days. We learned a harsh lesson from this exercise.

Both the biggest and best education we received was very early on in the treatments, when we were waiting for Martin to be readmitted. A well-built man with a beard walked through. The reception nurse said to us, "That's Peter, he's been off treatment a year now". Suddenly the spark of realisation hit me - 'blimey, we can do this - Martin can be cured!' It was the first time I thought there really was hope, and from that moment on I would not allow myself to believe anything other than the fact that big bro' was going to get better. I told mum and dad about it as their generation only knew cancer as a death sentence - they needed this hope too.

Martin suffered the usual side effects from the chemo. He lost his hair, but soon discarded his cap, getting used to the skinhead he was sporting. Mum had secretly collected some hair from his pillow for her locket, to keep a bit of him ever close. One of his feet was forever sweating, an odd sensation so he says. The sickness followed later. It seemed that as the treatment progressed and the chemo had less cancer cells to attack, so it took more out of the rest of his body.

He was guinea-pig for a new cannabis-based anti-sickness drug, but declined that after side effects meant he lost bladder control.

Whenever anyone talks about cancer, my first and foremost thought for the victims is of the 'positive mental attitude' that is so essential, and truly does make a difference. Martin gained huge confidence while on treatment - the little worries in life had paled into insignificance. He would come home from hospital and rush straight down the pub or cricket ground with his mates. He tried in vain to keep up pint for pint, but what mattered was that he was doing normal things again for a while.

On Christmas Eve 1985, we had been to the local pub and everyone came back to my house. Martin was three sheets to the wind and when he left to walk home I got a couple of his friends to follow at a distance - I wasn't about to see him run over after all he'd been through.

Martin, we soon discovered, was the richest of men - if you count the number of true friends in his life as opposed to the pennies. They crawled out of the woodwork for him, rallied round him. He received a signed card from Liverpool Football Club that someone had sent off for on his behalf.

One day, thirteen of Martin's friends visited him (I'm astounded they were all allowed in). He was in his own room at that time - mercifully for the other patients' sakes. They sat on windowsills, the floor, anywhere they could find. A poor nurse came in and took his blood pressure amidst the enclave. As she pumped the armband, so Martin puffed out his cheeks and body as if she was inflating him with air. His friends started falling off their perches with laughter.

Ever the clown and master of the 'one-liners', Martin did much to endear those around him, including using his drip-stand as a skateboard in the corridors. I remember him eagerly telling us about bumping into Sebastian Coe (now Lord Coe) in the lift one day.

Martin had a few tricks up his sleeve to enable him to get home quicker after courses of chemo. You aren't allowed home if you are still being sick, so he took to diving into the bathroom if he needed to retch. He also perfected the art of speeding the drips up so that the drugs administration was slightly quicker - I've no doubt they knew what he was up to, but his indomitable spirit won the day. He had such character, such guts - a real star. I admire him immensely.

Unlike today, in those days, there was little awareness of the necessary support for families of cancer victims. We knew nothing of cancer until it was in our midst. I read Bob Champion's book to try and get some guidance, scaring myself in the process. Julie and I were lucky that our bosses and work colleagues were very understanding.

The police force has always been excellent when you have issues within your family to overcome and Inspector Jeff Thompson, was my saving grace. He was so supportive and I will always be eternally grateful to him. There wasn't a minute of every day – or so it seemed - that my thoughts didn't drift to Martin.

Police work and shifts are pretty unforgiving at such times and I found myself dealing with the frequent delivery of agony messages and coping with sudden deaths at a time when my compassion was completely spent. I felt I couldn't give of my best to others, and just hoped I didn't let anyone down. I also regularly went forty-eight hours without any sleep when on night-shift due to it coinciding with returning Martin to Charing Cross or collecting him. I guess we all find the reserves when we have to.

On one occasion Martin was asked to speak to a seventeen-year old who was refusing more treatment and for whom there was no hope without it. As Martin said, you have no choice - if you want to live, you have to get on with it. He spoke to many others on a similar vein during his treatment.

Towards the end of his treatment Martin was told that his blood markers were back to normal. Scans still showed a one-inch lump on the stomach but this, they were sure, was dead tissue. They could operate to remove the lump for it to be analysed and confirmed as dead, or leave it there. He opted for the operation, during which they administered chemo to prevent any spillage of live cancer cells: a spillage means it could settle elsewhere in his body and reproduce, so this was vital.

The operation wasn't an easy one - they had to move his stomach and genital organs to get to the lump, but analysis of the tissue taken found that it was indeed dead and that the chemo had successfully beaten the cancer. The resultant operation scar was around a foot in length.

One sad side to having had the difficult operation and the cancer was that Martin was unable to have any children - another cruel blow for him and Julie who would have been fabulous parents.

I remember vividly when Martin had his Hickman line removed. The doctor literally had to kneel on his chest and tug like mad. I could hear him saying 'Heave ho' from behind the curtain. It didn't sound like much fun to me.

When Martin told mum that he no longer needed any more chemo, she cried for the first time in front of him since the onset of the whole nightmare. God knows, we'd all shed plenty of tears along the way. Martin had cried for us, we'd cried for him - the offloading is a good healer, and helps to sustain you at such times.

Martin returned to work in March 1986, having had fifteen full courses of chemotherapy, eight of which were the platinum treatment 'cisplatin' a very powerful, toxic drug. He married Julie on 31st May - it was a highly charged, emotive day. I had a dance with him to the Liverpool football song "You'll Never Walk Alone" by Gerry and the Pacemakers. The words are so true and the record is forever 'Martin's'.

As his metabolism returned to normal so he gained weight - the Mars bars now sitting on his waistline. He started running to shed any excess bulk. I did a parachute jump in November raising £4,250 for the Cancer Research Campaign (who ironically funded Mr Newlands). It was good to feel like we were giving something back to the man himself. Martin bought me a bottle of champagne on the night we handed over the charity cheque. The cork from the magnum has stayed with me ever since – it is my talisman, although has not *always* saved me from disaster.

The following year Martin ran the Berkhamsted half-marathon. As I watched him cross the finishing line I found it very moving - I was so proud of him I wanted to cry - I pictured him in that wheelchair and in a very different world.

Over the next eleven years Martin ran five London marathons. He has raised a lot of money for cancer charities and wears a Lance Armstrong yellow wristband (Lance has won six Tour de France cycle races and had survived the same testicular cancer).

The pattern of regular check-ups began, with blood tests, alternating between West Herts and Charing Cross hospitals. Mr Nicholls, gratified to see Martin so well, confided in him that when they had first met he considered him to be a 'dead man'.

The gap between check-ups lengthened each year until they were just annual routines. There was the odd major scare, like when Martin was recalled as his white cells were abnormal. It turned out that the heavy cold he had at the time of the time had affected the readings - everything was as it should be - he could breathe again!

Life returned to normal and so continued for twelve clear years, until January 1998 when another problem arose. One of Martin's testicles had hardened up. The now Professor Newlands at last knew the source of the primary cancer. An operation was carried out to remove the offending testicle. It had contained another tumour, but this time it was confined to the testicle and successfully removed…. so we thought!

Monthly check-ups returned and towards the end of that year Professor Newlands asked Martin if he was having any back pain. By the question alone Martin immediately knew there was something wrong – he had also been feeling below par, although not with back pain. It transpired that he again had cancer - for the *third* time.

Unfortunately, during the removal of the testicle in January there had been a live cell spillage. This had settled on a node at the back of Martin's stomach and so developed into his latest cancer - a seminoma, which thankfully wasn't an aggressive cancer like the teratoma fourteen years earlier.

Professor Newlands couldn't believe how unlucky Martin had been. Between Christmas and New Year he again found himself back on chemo. I had never seen him so depressed. There was no way through to lift his spirits. It was terrifying to think that it was all happening again. You tried so hard not to think 'What if this is it?' 'Is it going to get him this time?' You simply have to shut those thoughts away and get on with it.

His friends rallied again, this time he received a Liverpool FC shirt in the name of the then youngster 'Steven Gerrard' - both he and Martin have come a long way!

After four more courses of chemo he was told they may then use radiotherapy. He sat with Julie in a consultation room after his latest scans. They were to discuss the impending radiotherapy. Professor Newlands was then called into the room to look at the scans. He stood there shaking his head. Martin and Julie were rigid with anxiety. Professor Newlands looked again at the scans, turned to Martin and said "It's all gone". Martin's cancer had been completely eradicated. There was no need for any radiotherapy. It was agreed that they would give him one last course of chemo as double insurance - he would then be free to get on with living.

Out of the total five courses of chemo this time around, three were cisplatin (taking his grand total of chemo to twenty full courses, of which eleven were cisplatin -a total of one hundred and thirty-two hours of the most toxic drug around).

It is unusual for someone to have this much hard chemo, but Martin was an exceptional case. His only good fortune in this is that his body responded so well to it.

As I write today Martin has been all clear again for almost nine years. There is no good reason for the cancer to return. He has run two more marathons - completing the Edinburgh marathon just six months after coming off chemo - not a clever idea, but darned plucky all the same. He only runs now for his enjoyment and general fitness.

What can we say about Professor Newlands - how can you thank the man enough? He was tireless in his efforts in the treatment of cancer victims. Our entire family owes him a debt of gratitude – he has our utmost respect and will never be forgotten. Martin, I know, holds him in great esteem and with real affection. Mr Nicholls sent a very touching personal letter to Martin when he heard he was back on chemo. The caring profession truly does care! The nursing staff were simply amazing without exception.

Martin and I had quite a few heart to heart chats over the months of his first treatment – reminiscing on our childhood and underlining our close, unbreakable bond. I cherish these talks and am glad we took the opportunity to let each other know how much we needed and cared for each other.

We sadly lost dad in January 1997 before the cancer returned for a second and third time - it was even harder on mum this time around. I guess to have had cancer three times since the age of twenty-six is pretty rare. I know that Martin's medical notes are a mile thick and he has been a much-visited case study for student doctors. Martin at least was lucky enough to be in his own country. He saw patients from abroad who had no visitors at all. We at least could be there for him.

I heard someone once say "We knew nothing about cancer before, and we still wish we knew nothing about it". I understand that sentiment fully, except, I feel there are stories of inspirational survivorship that can give such hope to others. I hope this account is one such story.

Whilst Martins' case notes may weigh a ton - 'he ain't heavy…he's my brother!'

Somewhere Over the Rainbow

Martin Dec 1985   Martin's 1st half marathon   Wedding May 1986

Martin today   Martin's medal tally

Parachute Jump October 1986   With Martin & charity cheque

CHAPTER 9

THAT WAS THE WEEK THAT WAS

I miss you so, wish words could tell
Just what I feel each day -
Dear Dad, how much I love you.
That's all I need to say

Have you ever wondered at the mysterious events that occur at or around the time of a loved one's death? The week leading up to my own dear father's passing on 16th January 1997 was extraordinary to say the least, as were the episodes that ensued.

Dad was admitted to hospital on Sunday 13th January having had a heart attack. I decided to stay with mum until he was well enough to return home. On Tuesday morning I left early for work in frost and mist. Some ten minutes into my journey I was involved in a multiple car crash on sheet ice, writing my car off and acquiring a sporty surgical collar. That afternoon, with mum and Martin, I visited dad in hospital.

Dad always enjoyed a little flutter on the horses, which in the main were hapless, but he had a rare £10 winning bet to be collected from the bookies – he asked Martin to do the honours - it turned out to be an onerous task. That afternoon was to be our last time together as a nuclear family.

On leaving the ward that day, we turned and caught dad watching us. In unison we all raised our arms in farewell, thankfully, not realising the finality of the situation.

I view my accident as a blessing because it meant I was at home with mum early the next morning when the hospital rang requesting our attendance - those immortal words "Can you come to the hospital, your husband's not so well this morning"? In our hearts we knew that dad had moved on, which sadly proved to be the case.

Even before the funeral had arrived, the peace lily I had bought them some time ago burst into flower for the first time.

Dad's vegetable patch - still stocked, provided the next event. For years he had tried, and failed dismally, to grow cauliflowers. You can imagine our astonishment at the emergence of a cauliflower over one foot in diameter. It was such a revelation that I photographed mum holding the 'monster'. How proud dad would have been - he could have dined out on that one for months - literally!

Mum decided she would have to move from the big, cold house she was now rattling around in. A few years back dad had approached a neighbour, asking for first refusal on a maisonette that her parents were living in and that he had just decorated. Dad said it would be perfect for them in later life, but, in truth he would never have moved unless forced to. I made tentative enquiries with the neighbour. Ironically her parents were in the process of going into a nursing home and the maisonette became available shortly afterwards. Mum moved in that summer with dad's paint and wallpaper surrounding her. We can't help feeling that he hand-picked this home for mum's future.

Having written my car off in the accident I took over the running of dad's car. One day, soon after my Uncle Rod had died I got into the car and was greeted with the unmistakeable whiff of dad's Brylcreem hair lacquer – a sign I felt, that all was well. In 2004 I reluctantly traded the car in – doing so on 18th September - dad's birthday. I felt his presence and protection in the car until the day I parted with it and beseeched his spirit to follow me into my new vehicle!

There is quite simply nothing that can prepare you for losing a parent - they have been a constant force in your life from birth.

Dad was an old school 'character' with a wonderful sense of humour and fun. He was almost childlike in his enjoyment of the simple things in life – a quality to be envied as we all strive in this technological world of today to find some semblance of satisfaction.

Dad was a peaceful man who would do no-one any harm, despite having a short fuse, which he kindly handed down to me. He was no academic and often got words muddled providing us with much hilarity. I always thought the 'mollyment' was another of his mispronunciations of the Bridgewater Monument at Ashridge – until Bert Hosier, in 'Hedgehog's Northchurch' called it by the same name. I laughed with Bert about this and thus apologise dad, for once you got it right – in your old Northchurch dialect. Bert told me he would have loved a voice recording of dad as he had been one of the few villagers who really retained the dialect. Words like 'lobbo' (meaning 'watch out!'), 'puggled' (meaning mad, daft), and 'skedaddle' (meaning 'hurry up') were in general use. 'Watcha' and 'Ow-do' were common greetings, yet he always used formal 'Mr & Mrs' terms of address to those he felt to be of a higher social class than himself – even to one of our next-door neighbours! He had respect and always exercised it.

Neither was dad scared to be the butt of the jokes and fun. He enjoyed a good belly laugh and provided us with many – like one occasion when Liverpool Football club were on the television. As a true 'reds' household when Liverpool scored everyone cheered – dad and Martin jumped out of their seats. As dad landed, he forgot he was in the rocking chair and the whole thing tipped over backwards. Dad lay there with his feet flapping in the air, having damaged mum's fireguard, and totally helpless with a fit of the giggles he couldn't move. Neither could anyone else move – they were crying with laughter!

Both Martin and I were blessed with dad's sense of humour – both of us are adept at 'one-line' witty ripostes when the need arises. Dad relished this banter and I recall one such occasion when I had him giggling in response to a throwback line I gave him. Basically he was telling Martin and I that he approved of the paths we were taking through life, except for one weakness each. He said to Martin "You drink too much!" and then to me "You smoke too much!" I swiftly replied "And you talk too much!"

As mentioned before, dad's frugality was a joke at home - although when he took early retirement by two years, he did start to take two holidays each year with mum. We were delighted for them and mum admits they were the best holidays they had ever shared together. I only wish dad would have spent a little more money in 'today' instead of keeping more back for 'tomorrow'. Of course, it is a hard balance to strike and something many of us struggle with - but sometimes tomorrow never comes and for many - they are left with regret and the longest words in the English dictionary - 'If only...'

Dad brought much laughter, joy and love to our lives. He was a great storyteller, especially after half a shandy! We will always love him, miss him and cherish his memory with a smile or joke. Even in death, dad gave us a few more stories to tell - small events, maybe, but ones that have afforded us great comfort!

Dad's death and Martin's illness made me vow I would not be left with regrets. It is something I have taken with me ever since and I am so thankful now that I did.

So what of mum - and the new life she was forced into against her dearest wishes? Well mum has been simply amazing. You will never meet a gentler woman - who hides well the inner strength of an ox.

We saw those inner reserves in abundance throughout Martin's illness - she is a determined lady. She has always been the mainstay of love in the household - as indeed many mothers are. She worries endlessly about her children - no matter what grand old ages we have become.

Mum was always the one for a cuddle - whereas dad didn't do 'emotions' in that way - no matter how much he loved us. I will always regret that I was never able to tell dad just how much I loved him and so formed another promise to myself. I vowed from now on that I would always ensure those I loved knew exactly how I felt.

Mum had to establish a completely new way of living. From controlling the finances to dealing with everyday occurrences - she has had a steep learning curve. Of course Martin and I have always been on hand to assist but we are so incredibly proud of her and the way she has taken herself forward into this new life. She has gained an independence and confidence that I would never have imagined possible - although I should have known all along this was how she would be.

I embroidered a cross stitch picture for her early on which now hangs in her hallway. On it are the words of that wonderful prayer 'God grant me serenity to accept what I cannot change, courage to change the things that I can, and wisdom to know the difference'. Mum says she cannot count the times she has stopped and read these words. It is one of those verses that can fortify you in moments of weakness and doubt - and something I have subsequently come to fully appreciate.

Mum's move into the maisonette was the best thing she ever did. She loves her new home and garden and spends hours pottering about in it. She enjoys cutting the grass, planting up her pots and keeps everything so well maintained and pretty.

Mum's adage from the moment of losing dad was 'start as I mean to go on'. She has never flinched from that, no matter how painful the experience. She is a great role model for anyone newly bereaved. Whatever your ghosts and fears - if you face them they cannot frighten you any more - better still, you put them to rest, overcome the difficulties and gain huge confidence and a sense of achievement.

Mum also overcame her trepidation of flying and now loves looking down on Mother Earth from the sky. This in itself has opened up a whole new world for her. She would never have quite enough confidence to fly alone, but it does mean that we have been able to expand holiday destinations, and for me, my little surprise mother-daughter trips with her each year will always include flying - if not she would surely be 'disappointed'. Having savoured the magic of Venice, the splendour of Prague and the astounding beauty of Switzerland a whole new world has been laid at her feet. Of course I, too, have enjoyed these trips immensely and take pleasure in their planning. As she is in her seventy-fifth year I feel that I want to give her at least one annual 'special memory' - it is the least I can do for a woman who has sacrificed so much for me throughout her life and who continues to shower me with love by the 'bucket load'.

The one thing about having such a fantastic mother is that you know you always have a good sounding block - there is no substitute for experience and the wisdom that comes with age. I am fortunate in that we have always been incredibly close. We can take problems to each other and are mutually supportive. Mum's backing for me and for Martin in everything we do is 'total'. Concerned only with our happiness at the expense of all else, she has an unconditional love that has no bounds.

Having so nearly lost Martin, I appreciate he is *extra* special to her - his life in itself is worth the world to her, as it is to all the family, but for mum, having watched her only son go to hell and back - well, I can only imagine the pain it caused her. Thus, when Martin fell ill again on two consecutive years after losing my dad, my fear of what this could do to our family, in particular to mum was magnified tenfold. My only wish now is that mum lives to a ripe old age - and most importantly - that Martin outlives her.

Linda Pottinger

Our Mothers
What is a mother? A very special breed
That nursed us from the very start when we were but a seed.

From pregnancy to giving birth our burden she will know,
She takes our weight as we pass through infancy and grow.

In all our teenage troubles she is constant, always there,
And in adulthood you find a friend never failing in their care.

She shares our load in daily life - she supports us when we're weak,
She encourages all our heart desires and the happiness we seek.

She knows us better than anyone; shares our joy and feels our pain,
When we fall she is there waiting to pick us up again.

We will always be her baby - she will always dry our tears
And proudly proclaim us as the child she
has nurtured all these years.

She gives herself so willingly and doesn't expect to take,
When all she does is borne of love and all for goodness sake.

Our mothers should be cherished, they are deserving of our best,
They have a gift so very rare - yes, we are truly blessed.
Thank you mum - I love you.

Somewhere Over the Rainbow

Dad - centre in cut off trousers!   Dad in the army   Mum aged 14yrs

Mum & dad July 1954   Dad holding the ball - Northchurch FC

Mum & monster cauliflower   Mum & dad's last holiday together

CHAPTER 10

THE POT OF GOLD

As I walked in my Garden of Eden you were beside me.
I felt your hand in mine as I climbed higher skyward,
Heard your voice on the breeze as I gazed round in awe.
I could see you in the beauty of the trees, splashes
of colour in an otherwise grey day.

I felt you in the kiss of the mist and rain;
I breathed you in with the scent of the bracken.
I opened my heart to you, reached out to you and you touched me.
Your smiling eyes were before me-
Your tenderness and warmth.
Your passion sent a shiver down my spine,
Body and soul merged in paradise.

It all seems so simple now,
When once life was an intricate web - unfathomable.
Us pleasure seekers need only love and
someone to share it, to belong,
To love and be loved,
To care and be cared for,
To find joy in the tangible beauty of God's Creation -
Where the song of the birds is music,
And the colour of flowers is art,
When the warmth of the sun touches your spirit
Or the sting of the hail makes you feel alive.
The wind in your hair clears your head,
The power of mountains humbles you.

When nature's answer touches your very
soul all you need is to share it...
With someone special...
With you.

Having spent most of my life in a hapless quest for love I had all but given up on this happening to me. As often is the case, just when I wasn't looking, there he was - white charger at the ready - enter Dick.

Dick Pottinger - or should I say, Richard, as his mother constantly reminds us was not a stranger to me. I had known him for some ten years, mainly when he was Detective Chief Inspector in Dacorum Division. He was the very best man manager I have ever worked for. He led by example and cared with a passion about protecting the vulnerable - the elderly, the young, anyone who was ever a victim. He went after criminals with zest and dogged determination and quite simply got things done. Many retiring officers have alluded to Dick as the 'best detective' they have ever known. He was a simply magnificent copper - but an even more special man.

Dick was born on 31st March 1948, the third son of John and Margaret (Peggy). They had John first, then Michael and a five-year gap before Dick arrived, followed by David a couple of years later. Dick and David were close, as were John and Michael due to their proximity to each other in terms of ages.

John tragically died in 1959, aged seventeen years old in a drowning accident at Rickmansworth Aquadrome - Dick was just eleven years old. Peggy and John succeeded in shielding their younger sons so well from the distressing events that Dick could scarcely remember much about it - he always said they must have been fantastic to handle the ordeal in the way they did - he appreciated so much their love and care. John's body was not found for two days - a heartbreaking moment for any parent.

Peggy's family originated from County Mayo, Ireland and moved to England in the 1870s, settling eventually in South Shields. Peggy was one of twelve siblings, two of whom died in infancy. Six siblings gradually emigrated to America, starting after the General Strike of 1926.

Peggy met John, at school and they became an item in 1934 when Peggy was nineteen years old. John had left school at fourteen years old, working for Smiths, meeting the paper train at 4 a.m. each day. He then took a plumbing apprenticeship until he was twenty-one years old. Employment was very hard to find so John cycled to London to get work, later returning north where he took a job as an engineer for the General Post Office in Sunderland. He married Peggy in 1939.

Unhappy working in Sunderland, Peggy suggested John could get a transfer elsewhere within the Post Office.

One evening, Peggy had been to the scullery to get a pint of milk. Whilst pondering on John's dilemma, she turned the bottle round and her eyes fell on the word 'Watford'. She turned to John and said "That's where we will go!" John told her not to be so daft - how could they make such a decision, based on a milk bottle? Peggy is nothing if not determined, and told him 'they were going' - and that was that!

John's transfer came through and off they went. It was not an easy transition - it was wartime and their first son was just one year old, with another on the way. Peggy got domestic work as a caretaker of a house in Watford. They lived on the premises until at last they could buy their first house.

Peggy remembers it well - she said "The walls were streaming with water and it was freezing cold but we didn't care, we were so happy we danced round the room". They never once regretted the move they made - Peggy recalls "It was the best thing we did". I for one agree - it was my good fortune that they did so - I always knew milk was good for you!

And so it was in 1994, that we had re-opened the old murder enquiry - that of Joan Macan - at Ashridge in 1988, known within the 'job' as Operation Olive and to which I have referred previously. New information had come to light which offered hope and thus we were back on the warpath.

At some point during the daily briefings, my feelings for Dick deepened - I couldn't put a finger on it, nor did I really know why - it just happened. I fell head over heels in love with him. As well as we got on, engaged in easy conversation and as I found, had so much in common, I could do nothing about it. Dick was in an unhappy marriage which came to an acrimonious end a year hence.

Many moons later, my phone rang one evening - only to hear Dick's voice on the other end. He came round for a chat, poured out a great deal of heartache and we talked into the early hours. I must have come a long way from the person Dick first saw, when he was a uniformed Inspector - in his opinion I was 'frivolous' in those days!

Dick had been married twice. His first marriage to Angela gave him two lovely sons, Steven and Neil whom he simply adored. Angela thankfully allowed him good access to the boys, so father and sons developed a good relationship and friendship - they were his rock in his hour of need - and in their twenties when I first got to meet them. He always laughed about the way they 'had him over' with their homework as youngsters. He would give them a book to read and test them on what they had read later. Of course, they just read the front and back covers so they could summarise - they were quite sharp! He would take the boys on holiday and give them a few pennies for the amusement arcades, only to find they went searching all the machines to find extra coins people had left behind. There are many little stories, all part of growing up - but it was lovely to see such a close bond between them.

My own broodiness for a family, having spanned some fourteen years or so, had passed. I was thirty-four years old when Dick and I came together, and I had no hankering for children by now. I am convinced that no-one can have everything in this world - I had what mattered most of all to me - Dick. While I may rue not having had a family, sharing my life with Dick meant far more to me and I will never have any regrets about that. I had also gained two friends in Steven and Neil so I had no complaints.

Dick's personal confidence had been shattered by his second marriage break-up - he knew his worth in a professional capacity, but regarded his personal life as having been a disaster. We took things incredibly slowly and I exercised a patience I never knew I possessed in allowing him to come to terms with what had gone before, and to look ahead to a future, in which I would be there for him always.

Rebuilding his fragile self-confidence and gaining his complete trust was understandably difficult. I knew from the start that this man was the special one for me - that no matter how long it took, nor how many obstacles were before us, I would not let him down - not for one minute.

I helped Dick with his move to a bungalow in Bricket Wood, together with some good friends, Ron and John, and Steven and Neil.

I bought him a bird house/table as a house-warming present. He loved that bird table - it was rustic for a start - which was to his taste - but he admitted what he loved most was the fact I had bought it for him - his home - not trying to assume I would be there with him all the time - in short I was giving him the breathing space he badly needed.

We developed a pattern for seeing each other - I would come over on Saturday, stop a night and be back home ready for work on Monday. Over the months this gradually increased so that I would be there from Friday evening to Monday morning - but the process was very gradual. I was not going to overcrowd him until he was ready.

I remember well the first time Dick cooked a meal for me. Well, actually it was the third meal - he had already delivered two splendid breakfasts which he claims were to 'woo' me - but since I was already madly in love with him, he could have saved himself all that washing up. He asked Kathy, the cook at Watford Police Station how to make Boeuf Bourguignon and so this culinary delight was served. It was delicious, although the meat could have done with longer as it was a touch on the chewy side. With tweaking and practice he later perfected the dish - it became his pride and joy and our favourite Boxing Day meal - it was truly scrumptious.

Having slaved away on this meal for me you might think I would, at least, offer some form of reward - I intended to

- honest I did, but after such a feast and a few glasses of red wine I fell into a contented slumber. Dick - being chivalrous, thought it was lovely that I felt relaxed enough to sleep and claimed not to mind at all - hmm - I don't know as I would have been quite so generous!

We developed a penchant for giving each other special birthday surprises and one such event was early on in our relationship. Ron had started up a car-hire business for special occasions - he had stretch limousines and a white Rolls Royce. I had booked up to take Dick to see the musical Buddy at the theatre and hired the white Rolls Royce to take us - along with our friend John as the 'suited and booted' chauffeur. It was a spectacle far removed from that of the burly, maverick guy, with a somewhat 'rough cut' image. It provided the icing on the cake and a wonderful start to a great day out.

I did take one risk - or what others might perceive as a risk anyway. Dick's spare cash had run out and I knew how dearly he wanted a proper conservatory. I had just taken out a savings policy and wanted to do something for him - a special birthday present - not to mention an expensive one! Dick was away golfing for two days and I secretly arranged a window fitter I know to rip out the old conservatory windows and build a proper one. It was a challenge, but accomplished well, and I had just finished painting and arranging the furniture that I had stored at mum's with about an hour to spare before he returned home. He must have wondered why I had asked to greet him on his return - but as it was his birthday I got away with it.

I did have a little trepidation that Dick might see this as me trying to buy my way into his house, but I knew differently - I knew we were meant to be, yet regardless of that I wanted to do this one kindness for him. He had been through so much and it was my way of helping.

When he got home his face was a picture as I led him into his new conservatory. It took a while for the penny to drop as at first he had thought I had just bought the furniture.

As he looked around and saw the whole gift he was totally speechless. It was so worth it just to see his delight.

When my dad went into hospital I went to stay with mum - the intention being that I would be with her until he came home from hospital, which of course did not happen. Dick came to visit dad in hospital and was so kind to mum and supportive of me when dad died. I didn't get to see him properly for over two weeks until one day when Martin and Julie had mum to stay over a night and I went to catch up with Dick again.

Only a few short months later mum put her house on the market as she was buying her maisonette. Then the unthinkable happened - Dick asked me to move in with him! Well, I should have been dancing in the streets and shouting from the rooftops!

I was delighted of course, but the thought of helping with mum's house sale at the same time as trying to sell mine was a tall order - so I asked if we could wait a little while until mum was settled. Dick later confessed to me that the fact I dropped everything to support and care for my mother had impressed him. He adored his own mother and recognised the same spirit within me. It convinced him that I was 'for real' and so our unbreakable bond was forged.

After a few weeks I thought I should get the house valued - it would take a while to sell after all! The day the estate agents came round to measure up, so did my buyer - they bought it there and then. Yikes - this wasn't supposed to happen so quick - thus mum and I were selling at the same time. Thankfully I had a period of grace between us both moving homes!

The day I moved in a large bouquet of flowers were delivered with a 'Welcome to your New Home' tag attached - it was a thoughtful, loving touch. I felt I had indeed come 'home' at last.

Having lived alone for fourteen years, I suspected it would be hard readjusting to sharing my life - the whole 'kit and caboodle' and in losing my space - but I needn't have worried.

From the moment I moved in it was like putting on a pair of comfortable slippers - we belonged together. The only minor adjustments we had to make were in our respective body clocks. I was always an early to bed - early to rise person, whereas Dick was the night owl who preferred to sleep in at weekends. To begin with I stayed up later than normal, and he would get up earlier than he wanted to. We decided we should just carry on as normal - and so it worked. Dick would sit in the armchair with his newspaper, checking shares late at night or watching a film, while I would turn in with a good book. It was an ideal compromise - that way we both had room for ourselves - something we all need.

I initially found it hard allowing Dick to pay for me all the time - from meals out to weekend breaks. In my independent former life I had been so used to 'paying my own way' that I found it difficult - as if I wasn't 'contributing'. It did get easier gradually and of course we pooled resources - everything was 'our money' not mine or Dick's. We never hid pay packets from each other like some folk do - we were a partnership with equal shares and an equal voice.

Dick asked me if I minded him going to his 'Friday Club' - which comprised mainly of former work colleagues who met in a St Albans pub every week. Why should I mind? It gave me the chance to have a leisurely slob in an aromatherapy bath, watch TV, play music or do whatever I felt like doing.

He also checked if it was okay to go away on the occasional golf trips with friends. I was touched that he asked, but of course I never minded at all. It was great to have time apart as well as together and meant we always had new things to talk about. I never got possessive about Dick's time in that way - it was healthy to have some freedom. Similarly, I would go to mum's once a week, leaving him to fend for himself. The security of knowing we would always be coming home to each other made it so special.

There were some occasions when Dick was pulled in so many directions by others, always putting himself last, that I did voice my concerns. His work with the charity West Herts

Against Crime was one such pull. Dick had been with the charity from its inception in 1995, thus it had always been part of our life together. He later became Chairman, and remained so until October 2006.

He was dedicated to a fault and cared so much about its work - in helping victims of crime, the elderly and vulnerable to be secure in their homes. He even donated some of his hard-earned police pension to the charity on his retirement in 1998 at a time when they had severe funding difficulties. He was tireless and focused in his quest to help others – such was his compassion for people.

Whenever we went to a function together, Dick attracted people like a magnet - they all wanted a piece of him. We would often part in the entrance, only to see each other again as we were leaving. It was heart-warming for me to watch, knowing that other people loved him so much too - I was incredibly proud of him. Yes, at times I wished I could spend more time with him at such events, but I was lucky - I got to go home with him, to share my life with him - I felt so privileged.

We both left the police force in May 1998. Dick retired having served thirty-one years. I had completed eighteen years service and left due to the fact that I wanted to devote my time to getting the maximum out of life with Dick – after all, he would be sixty-two years old by the time I had completed my full thirty years service. Having learned from losing my father at sixty-five years old, and the experiences with my brother's ill health, it was an easy, but important decision to make. It proved to be the best move I ever made.

Dick loved police work and I thought I would have to batten down the hatches - that we could be in for a bumpy ride. Making adjustments after such a demanding job - and having been on call for the large part of the previous thirteen years or so, was likely to be tough. It was another key factor in my decision to quit - if I stayed, then Dick would always have a boot in the camp. As it happened, I need not have been so concerned - although he missed the people, he didn't miss the 'job'.

Dick had enjoyed a thoroughly rewarding career but was ready for the next chapter in his life to commence. It was time for new pastures for both of us and started with our love of travel.

I had four months leisure time then took a part-time administrative support job in Watford. It was a strange sensation having my first job interview since the age of sixteen. Having left school with nothing but 'O' levels I was worried about creating a Curriculum Vitae that lacked other academic qualifications. I hadn't appreciated that policing skills, when converted onto paper, make very powerful reading and I always received interviews for anything I have pursued.

I was happy to empty my head of police intelligence work and prepared to get bored for a while. I missed the income, but adjusted, until in spring 1999 I decided to go self-employed. A few flyers placed around local business parks came up trumps so I quit the administration job to work for myself. I took manual and Sage bookkeeping courses to add to my armoury. Professionally, it is like watching the paint dry in comparison to police intelligence and to this day I miss the buzz I got from that role, but I have made good friends in my new working life, including my first ever clients - David and Jan. I work for some really nice people, have variety and it pays the utility bills.

What I miss most is the reward that comes from doing a job that 'makes a difference' to society - the giving back to communities and doing something fundamental to help others in their daily lives. Of course, people need their accounts finalising and naturally it helps them, but the contrast in working for profit-making companies as opposed to working for the 'good of all' is massive - it is far less fulfilling. I would like to think one day, as a volunteer I will be able to give back to society again.

Dick took eight months off before working for St Albans Council as Community Safety Officer. He didn't attain fulfilment from the role, finding that getting things done within local authorities was even harder than in the police force. Naturally he had some clout in the police, could make things happen and worry about any 'fallout' after the job was done and the mission accomplished. With the council there were too many tiers of structure to fight through and he was increasingly frustrated.

Dick aspired to be a landscape gardener - to do something totally different. I found an advert in the local paper for a jobbing gardener and, together, we went to take a look. The job was for an elderly farmer with a large area of land. He kept horses, grew vegetables and required a high degree of maintenance. Dick immediately hit it off with the landowner and so started on his gardening venture. It was to be the precursor for his landscaping work. Former colleagues soon got to know what Dick was doing and asked him to design and landscape their gardens.

Work flowed for the next few years and Dick gave up most of the maintenance jobs to concentrate on this more challenging aspect. It was what he loved most and it was a gratifying to see him come home, exhausted, fulfilled and thrilled by his achievements. Dick relished his new venture and failed to disappoint his customers. Moreover, he was always very reasonable in what he charged - often far too cheap - but he was happy and trouble-free.

With the gardening work came another of Dick's favourite pastimes - his wallow in the bath before our evening meal as he washed away the day's mud and eased his aching muscles. He came to love the bath as much as his bed and it became a standing joke that the phone had to go in with him as it always rang, as if on cue. He would curse my frequent interruptions, to share the news of the day or ask him something - I created a draught with the door opening and closing all the time - but it was sometimes the only time I could get his attention and know he had no escape!

Naturally as one gets older, the body takes any knocks a bit harder and it just so happened as Dick laid the final paving slab in a friend's garden that his back popped out. He acquainted himself with a good osteopath, and the landscape gardening became history in terms of a profession. It was well-timed, coinciding with the demand for work drying up. He had also become involved in ad hoc work for a Corporate Investigation Company - Outforce, which was set up by some of his former work colleagues. So it seemed, as one door closed another one opened.

Dick was happy to be at the hub of investigative work again and basked once more in the camaraderie of his workmates and the challenge the tasks presented.

While our working lives were, of course, important - our personal life together was sacrosanct. Dick and I were lucky - we were so compatible in every way. We spent hours chatting at the meal table on a Saturday evening, discussing everything and anything. We loved music and played endless CDs as we chatted - interrupted by Dick's occasional 'Meat Loaf' impression, drumming the table and playing air guitar as "Bat Out of Hell" resounded'. Being a home bird, I always enjoyed those evenings at home more than going out. It was great to socialise with friends but even better to have quality time together - we had a good balance of each.

We both had our own separate interests. While I enjoyed writing, and more recently trying to teach myself Italian, Dick loved his golf. Most times he would return from a hard day on the fairway, having had a poor or indifferent game, but he invariably had fun, a laugh and total enjoyment. He had some great days to remember - particularly in June 2006 when he won a tournament and came home beaming from ear to ear.

There were always little gems to tell me from his golf trips - the banter had obviously flowed together with the booze - if anyone had done something daft they were the butt of the jokes - like the time Derek with his in-car 'satellite navigation' managed to end up many miles in the opposite direction to that intended. Dick wasn't perfect and provided the entertainment one year when he managed to go to France and back on my passport - having taken it by mistake!

Linda Pottinger

Dick's smile and laugh were one of the things I adored most - his smile could melt ice and his laugh was highly contagious. How I love that laugh!

We, of course, had shared loves – mainly our garden, travelling and, most certainly, each other.

Our Garden

How many gardeners toiling away working fingers down to the bone
Have ever paused to consider the mating life of a stone?

Just how is it when you thought they had
gone, others are found in their place?
As you plunge in the fork with all you possess,
jangling nerves as you yell and
grimace.

It's always the one spot the prongs need to go
that resistance is met mighty hard -
Makes me wonder just how they reproduce and
why aching, my joints are all jarred.

So I sweat and dig on, I will not be beat - by
the pebbles, the granite or flint -
That are breeding in soil beneath my feet
as my cheeks turn a rosier tint.

I beg for a clue of where they're hiding away
- my patience and energy spent;
And while they lie in their beds making whoopee-
the tools of my trade are all bent.

I helped Dick planning and creating his garden from scratch when he moved into Bricket Wood - or rather - I helped with the donkey work!

Dick was the creator, and over the years the creation has changed, developed and been tweaked continuously - in part due to the high water table, which affected what plants were suitable - but also on account of evolving new ideas. Gardening is a never-ending, forever growing pleasure in which you can totally immerse yourself - it does wonders for the soul.

There was an old orchard at the bottom of the garden, a round concrete-walled overgrown pond, with a straight concrete path leading up to the former 'old curiosity shop' type conservatory.

A pre-fab garage was sited near the bungalow with an old office/shed at the side. All of these features were ripped out. The shed was reduced by a third and moved by Ron and John. I helped Dick in digging out the concrete and barrowing earth until my arms and legs dropped off. Straight lines in a garden were a 'no, no' for Dick - and certainly they aren't aesthetically pleasing on the eye. The paths and pond had to go, and Tony, Ron's brother laid a patio with wonderful curved edging.

For a slightly-built lass I was strong, but never knew my limitations therefore I was forever overloading the wheelbarrow - only for it to tip over, taking me with it. It caused much hilarity between us. As in my 'little red welly' years, I revelled in being plastered from top to toe in mud.

Our friends helped us take a dangerous section of very tall conifer down at the bottom of the garden. We were all lined up taking the strain of the rope, like a tug of war team, as the chainsaw was put to work on the trunk. When the tree was ready to fall everyone shouted 'now' and ran away dropping the rope - I say everyone, except me of course, being totally oblivious as to what I should do. I just fell flat on my back in the mud, wellies akimbo, and was very fortunate that the tree missed me!

We worked tirelessly in the garden every weekend and gradually things took shape. It is now most wonderfully mature and a delight to be in. There are little wooden walkways or log stepping stones separating areas of lawn, with every section feeling like a different room, offering another view. It entices you to walk around and explore further. Dick built pergolas and rustic fences. The compost heaps are secreted at the bottom of the garden and we have four, much needed water butts.

While Dick was the creator and designer, I was the 'plants person' and as in all things we complimented each other, becoming the very best of teams working with our respective strengths and weaknesses.

More recently we laid gravel seating areas in spots where plants were hardest to get going. I'm particularly pleased with these features as they were actually my idea!

Dick's roses are legendary - not so much for their brilliance, but for the fact he refused to have a rose without scent. He always said "A rose without perfume is no rose at all", which is why a stroll round the garden can take an age, as you stop to cup blooms in your hands and breathe in their delicious aroma. For us both there is nothing so evocative of a sultry summer's day than the sweet scent of flowers and shrubs. They transform the garden into a haven of peace and tranquillity. Today the virtues of aromatherapy are widely appreciated - as gardeners we have much in our armoury to soothe the soul and restore the equilibrium.

We have been rewarded in abundance by the roses we possess - they have never ceased to perform. I love the way that, as rosebuds open with the deepest hue at the core, the outer petals fade with age and sunshine, giving a perpetual, ever-changing blend of colours.

It is important to use colour effectively in a garden - we favoured pastel flowers - pinks, whites and blues with striking, more flamboyant colours confined to the patio pots or baskets. We have attained that 'cottage garden' feel that we both adore.

The diversity of our shrubs has added to the interest and gives all-year-round shape and form. Dick also had a special love of clematis and thus I had to learn the pruning regime for each variety.

Maintenance of the garden was quite another issue - not one of Dick's strong points. Yes - pruning was his forte - but no, he never tidied up after himself - that was left to me - trundling along behind gathering the clippings in his wake, huffing and puffing at his untidiness as I went. Since gardening became Dick's profession, keeping our own plot ship-shape landed firmly in my lap - it was too much of a busman's holiday for him. I almost always cut the grass, which, with five areas of lawn to deal with is easier said than done.

In keeping with our garden we also had birds nesting each year - until the cat arrived next door. We had blackbirds and robins either side of the kitchen window amidst the honeysuckle. We could stand and watch them on the nest from inside the kitchen. We both loved the birds and as with all other wildlife we found it captivating.

So the garden has been our passion - I have never felt more 'at one' with Dick than when working in the garden - no matter that we might be at opposite ends. It is a closeness I cherish dearly - and in any garden he is 'with me'.

Travelling

We celebrated our departure from the police force by taking a couple of fabulous holidays. Dick had always wanted to travel and I shared this love. Dick would tell me what to pack for our trips to prevent my usual desire to take everything!

We went to the lovely island of Tobago, in the Caribbean, leaving all our cares behind us - simply unwinding and relaxing. One cloudy day we decided to take a walk to the neighbouring resort. As we approached I recognised a man on the footpath ahead. It was Wilf, a man who thirteen years earlier had run a sports shop in Berkhamsted. He had moved, some six years previously, to Blackpool. Wilf is Trinidadian and was over visiting family, when he and his wife decided to pop across to Tobago for a break. It wasn't to be the only time Dick and I had amazing chance encounters in far-flung places.

Two months later we took a stunning Norwegian Fjords cruise. We had immense fun with a group of Scots on this cruise - and astonishingly in January 2003 we bumped into two of these Scots, Bill and Mary Cunningham while in New Zealand. It was an amazing and quite unbelievable coincidence. I swear the world is shrinking!

The following January we went to Thailand and, ironically, on the same tour as someone we knew in the police force. We particularly enjoyed people-watching at the bustling floating market, and the River Kwai region. Going on the Death railway and seeing Hellfire Pass and the museums was a very moving, humbling experience. The surrounding countryside is quite beautiful and a fitting shrine for those poor men who lost their lives in the war. To work in the extreme heat with bare hands, crude tools and nothing more than a loin cloth for protection against the sun beggars belief. It is a wonder anyone came out of there alive - it is a hostile environment for anyone engaged in hard labour, let alone those treated without mercy and humanity.

Dick and I were cross with a woman on the tour who was scathing about two seventeen-year old Japanese youths, who like us, were there to bear witness to these past events. In her bigoted opinion they had no right to be there as they were 'Japanese'! We were appalled at her attitude and admired the youngsters for their courage and friendship when faced with such a 'hostile foreigner'. They were no more accountable for the actions of their ancestors than we were!

In February 2000 we went to the Maldives - such heaven. The islands are exquisite - real postcard material. I used to think postcards had been touched up until I saw the depth of colours for myself. The white coralline sand, clear turquoise and deep blue waters and vivid blue skies were a dream. Lazy palm trees bowed down before the waters in homage. The snorkelling was amazing, with waters festooned with an array of spectacular, coloured fish of all shapes and sizes.

From the resort islands and deserted islands to locally inhabited islands it is the most romantic destination and it just happened to be a leap year! So, as faint heart never won gorgeous man, I decided I would propose to Dick - well it was the best chance of him saying 'yes', being in such divine surroundings. It didn't elicit quite the romantic response I was praying for.

What I actually got was "Well I'm not saying no" - to which I responded "Is that a yes then?" "It's more a case of how!" he replied. As a divorced Roman Catholic, a church wedding was off limits for Dick; neither of us wanted a registry office as they are so impersonal - so my task when we got home was to find the 'How' which I will come onto later.

Other travelling took us to some wonderful places. We went to India and Sri Lanka, although both of us suffered at the hands of the food in Rajasthan - I guess the monkeys that kept sneaking the food weren't washing their hands first, and we paid the price for their nasty germs. Again, the countryside is beautiful, although in areas such as Agra, near the Taj Mahal there is such abject poverty that it would be a brave person who walked along the streets alone. The forts were grandiose, but there is little done to maintain them and the entrances are littered with beggars - many being children, sickeningly maimed by their parents in their bid to elicit the odd coin from a visitor's pocket. The Taj Mahal, however, is quite magnificent - a true spectacle and I will never forget the first glimpse of this amazing edifice.

We have visited the United States on a couple of occasions - not just to visit our dear friends Rosie and Ric, but also to explore. It is a land of wonder with outstanding natural phenomena.

Dick joined me for two weeks of a month-long stay I had with Rosie when Ric was away on Air Force secondments abroad. Our relationship was in its infancy then, but we took a few days out together to see more of New Mexico. We visited White Sands National Monument, the beautiful Ruidoso and a small town called Cloudcroft, where a café actually still had sawdust on the floor. Dick was tense when we left for the trip - still unsure of his own standing in the world, and of me. It did wonders for him - he relaxed so much - and laughed mercilessly as a fat pigeon shed its load on my head - it was indeed lucky!

Rosie took us to the Grand Canyon - a mere twelve hours drive! I would not describe it as beautiful but it is truly awesome. I hoped to take a plane ride in the canyon as it was my birthday, but Rosie was having none of that - too many light aircraft are not regulated and operate at will. As it happens she was right. Within a day a plane had crashed taking the lives of all on board - British tourists no less. We drove on through the red rock areas and the gorgeous Sedona.

Dick and I went back to America just ten days after the horrific 911 terrorist attack on the World Trade Centre. The locals couldn't believe we had flown - America was in a state of shock. We flew into Denver and hired a car, taking us across Colorado, and down into the south east of Utah, past some incredible landscape at a place called Mexican Hat. I was desperate for a photograph stop but it was a clearway with no such permitted opportunity.

The geology of the land transfixed me - patterned and coloured like an Aztec blanket - it had a real 'Wow' factor. Canyonlands amongst other similar landscapes is another experience altogether - you can almost see the dinosaurs racing about, doing battle - it is quite spooky, but certainly majestic.

We drove into Arizona and Monument Valley - where, due to 911 there were rooms vacant at the coveted Goldings Lodge - in fact we could have our pick. The sunsets were sublime and we felt like stars in a John Wayne movie. We drove to Rosie's for a few days, before going back up to Colorado and the Rocky Mountain National Park, which is some 9,000 feet above sea level. The mountains are gargantuan and ominous. In the car we climbed to 14,000 feet above sea level - with some incredibly hairy drops to one side. The air was thinner, clearer and colder with each turn of the wheels. It was, however, not such a friendly place to be when fork lightning was crackling through the sky.

In 2003 we took an extended break of almost six weeks - stopping first at Singapore one night, before discovering Australia and new Zealand, and then to Bali for a week before returning home.

We made wonderful discoveries, such as the Kuranda rain forest and the Great Barrier Reef. We stayed a few days on the eco-friendly Fraser Island - with its less friendly dingoes and five of the most venomous snakes in the world. Being ever wary of the nasty little spiders Australia hosts, I must have checked under every loo seat before daring to perch my rump. We drove down the Pacific Highway - the coast road to Sydney - stopping off wherever we fancied - lovely spots such as Nambucca and Noosa Heads. We had the best ever fish and chip supper on the river bank in Noosa, where pelicans came up to us begging scraps.

Sydney was divine - the first view of the opera house, harbours and bridge was akin to our first sight of the Taj Mahal in India. It was time to stop, regroup a while and stand and gaze even longer. It was cosmopolitan, a hive of activity and quite lovely.

We went to the Blue Mountains, with a mystique of their own, despite the viewpoints being shrouded in mist.

We crossed over to New Zealand for a tour of the notoriously scenic South Island - again we weren't blessed with good weather. It was en route to the Milford Sound that we bumped into our Scottish friends from the Norwegian Fjords cruise.

We did have one fantastic, hot, clear-sky day in Queenstown and took the cable car up to the Skyline restaurant where the views are unparalleled. Dick rightly said, if there is one place where God exists, it is surely this - the most beautiful place on earth.

I watched with envy as I saw people paragliding in tandem with instructors. The conditions for this activity were posted as outstanding - and so it was that the pull of the attraction had me beaten. A perfect day, perfect place - now was the time to do such crazy things. It was such an exhilarating experience. As I left the safety of the mountainside the wind lifted us up over the strongly scented pine trees. It was an intoxicating blend.

The instructor kept me up circling over Queenstown for twenty minutes or so, and apart from having lost my wristwatch on take-off it was money well spent. I raced back to the cable car like a demented idiot for the ascent back up the mountain to Dick. I couldn't stop grinning - and was assured by the attendant 'they all look like you dear when they've done that'! Dick went on the go-karts, but I know he wished he had the nerve to paraglide. I don't know why he felt trepidation as I bought him a glider flight one Christmas and he absolutely loved the experience - maybe it was the vulnerability of having all that 'space' around you. Nevertheless it was a day to remember.

Bali was in a sorry state when we arrived there - it was only a few weeks since suffering the terrorist attack in the heart of their tourist trap. What is it with us that we go to areas a short time after such campaigns have struck? Maybe it is the safest time, I don't know!

The sweet Balinese people were struggling as their tourist trade had been decimated. We at least brought a smile to a few faces when we managed to lock ourselves out on the balcony of our room one morning, clad only in dressing gowns and had to be rescued by the cleaner!

This extended trip had been a real voyage of 'discovery' – and I have to say it didn't end when we came home.

Several weeks, if not months later, I went to use a match from a small box of matches I had picked up in the hotel in Sydney – either from our room or the reception area. As I opened it some plastic appeared. When I pulled on it, to my absolute horror I found I was holding a small cellophane wrap containing a whitish powdery substance! It had all the hallmarks of being something highly illegal. I shared this new 'discovery' with Dick, who was equally horrified and down the sink it went

– pronto! Doubtless it was a small 'deal' of drugs of some sort. I went cold when I thought of the potential outcome had this box of matches that I had carried around for a few weeks in my handbag been found. Australian airport security is really hot so I am amazed it wasn't picked up. I have visions of Balinese officials shouting 'off with her head' or being incarcerated in prison for years had it been found by their airport authorities. There was, of course, another potential hazard – that being the owner, or intended recipient of the 'deal'. What if I had been watched picking up the matchbox from a reception table – the consequences aren't too palatable are they? Of course I'm not a drug smuggler, dealer or any such thing – but just how would I have proved this to the authorities? Quite simply – I couldn't have proved anything – there it goes again - the cold sweat - perish the thought.

The moral of the story is to carefully check anything you pick up, no matter how innocuous a small box of matches is on the exterior. It proves things aren't always what they seem to be – I was just lucky that this 'wrap' wasn't found by anyone else except me.

We have enjoyed further trips abroad, such as Sharm El Sheikh in Egypt - the Red Sea again is like a massive aquarium and the coral is the prettiest of all I've seen. We explored parts of Europe and it was love at first sight when we went to Venice, hence why I simply had to take my mum there.

Italy is a country I want to see much more of, which is why I am trying to teach myself Italian - a lovely language with people to match.

Our last main exploration holiday was a wonderful cruise - or rather two cruises taken back to back. One was around the Greek Islands, and the other, some tasteful locations on the Mediterranean. The first cruise started and ended in Venice. We discovered Pompeii - a 'must see' place on anyone's itinerary. It has an aura all of its own, is so dramatically steeped in history and is quite fascinating. What you are privy to defies belief - I just wish I could see it around 8 a.m.

without the tourists - to be able to really 'feel' the place and 'breathe' it all in.

There was also the charming volcanic Greek island of Santorini, whose excavations and history are far older than Pompeii. The town of Oia is exquisite, with blue domed churches, white walls and spectacular sea views. The streets are a narrow, winding rabbit warren in which you could lose yourself forever.

We went through the Corinth canal (the ship fitting tightly in the narrow channel), stopped at Korcula, Croatia and when the trip ended at Nice we had a free excursion along the coast to Monaco - where Dick was in his element. The opulent yachts are gigantic - the mooring fees immense – a peek into another world, far removed from our own.

Aside from our more dramatic trips, Dick and I always took each other away for surprise weekends - principally on our birthdays. We stopped buying each other gifts - that way we both got a treat and could enjoy each other's company – the best present of all. In the true spirit of the adventure, Dick would employ subterfuge to fox me when going on these surprise trips. He would pull up to the front of one hotel, only to drive out again; or we'd have a quick stop in a lovely village, only for him to walk through the door of a hotel, pretend to look at tariffs, then suddenly announce our arrival to the receptionist. He had me fooled every time!

We uncovered fabulous romantic retreats in the United Kingdom - such as Symonds Yat; beautiful hotels - such as The Millstream at the fishing village of Bosham, and exquisite Cotswolds retreats such as Painswick, Burford and my beloved Castle Combe. We have taken a couple of trips to our favourite Exbury Gardens, Beaulieu and Lymington in the vicinity of the New Forest, and the neighbouring, much undervalued Isle of Wight. We also took in cities such as Bath, York and London, not to mention Barcelona and Rome.

All in all we have done a lot of exploring at home and abroad and at no time have we been disappointed - whatever the weather. We made the most of every venture as if it were our last - a good philosophy to have.

Being away together and finding joy in new places has held endless fascination for us - and the challenge of seeking out destinations has been fun. I concede that Dick was far better hunting for the perfect hideaways than me and somehow picked venues according to my mood or level of fatigue. He was brilliant at identifying need within me - it is something I loved so much about him.

Aside from our 'couples' weekends we had immense fun on the yearly 'mystery' weekend with our mothers - collectively referred to as 'the two mums'. Thankfully they got on well from the moment they met. I can still visualise Dick and I tentatively peering round the kitchen door, watching the 'two mums' in the conservatory. They had met only five minutes earlier. We watched with baited breath, sighing with relief as they 'jawed' nineteen to the dozen - and so it has been ever since. We have been extremely fortunate, unlike some friends who have to keep respective parents away from each other - that is so sad and such a loss. Peggy, Dick's mum, who is now almost a magnificent ninety-three years old and sprightly with it, has a very sharp brain - far too bright for a mother-in-law let me tell you!

Each year we planned a short two or three night stay somewhere. The 'mums' didn't know where they were going and we deliberately kept them guessing. Peggy would peep over my shoulder trying to steal a look at the road atlas - then they would try to work it out from the signposts - and were invariably wrong.

One April we took them to the Isle of Wight and thank the Lord had non-stop sunshine. As we pulled into the car park at Southampton's ferry terminal and latched on to the queues, Peggy thought we had stopped off at a car boot sale. I asked mum if she knew where we were going - looking smug she said "Well I think we're going on a ferry - there's one over there - look - but I've no idea where it's going!" Dick and I curled up - the only sign they had missed was the very large one at the entrance emblazoned in bold letters 'Red Funnel Isle of Wight Ferries'.

We have taken them to Austria, Bruges, Harrogate, Wells, Bath and Edinburgh amongst others and each trip got easier, more fun-filled and more hysterical as we went. People often say the generations don't mix - it simply was not so for us. Peggy and my mum are almost a generation apart in themselves and we found them fantastic company.

Our Wedding

Having been given the task in The Maldives to find out 'How' we could get married, I set about the internet with frenzied interest. There are, nowadays, numerous options - hotels, gardens - you name it - you can marry almost anywhere. I first thought about our own garden, but then decided it would be a bad idea as we might never feel free to move house. I then enquired about Exbury Gardens - although you would have to have a springtime wedding, so as to capitalise on the exquisite colours of the rhododendrons, azaleas and acers for the photographs. As it happened Exbury at that time wasn't licensed for marriages anyway.

Then I found it - the most idyllic hotel - and to think we had been to the village twice and never seen The Manor House at Castle Combe! As I gazed longingly at the computer screen I was already off into realms of fantasy - a fairytale wedding paradise and all within the most picturesque village I've ever seen. I printed off some pictures, chuckling - there was **no way** we would be able to afford this one!

Showing Dick, I anticipated a huge guffaw instead of the words that were music to my ears, "That's more like it!" he said. Well blow me down, I'd better find out more and quickly.

We decided on a very small wedding party - our two mums, my brother and sister-in-law, Dick's two sons and two sets of mutual friends. It wasn't cheap but affordable for such a special day and with a small party.

I made invitations and orders of service on the computer and wrote a poem for the ceremony called *'Gardening with Love'* - most appropriate for the two of us.

A certain amount of maturity is a good base on which to build;
Preparation of the soil and tilth for roots to flourish and yield.

Allow sufficient space to develop; nourish regularly I suggest;
Occasional pampering and pruning will
keep things looking at their best.

Have an element of intrigue to entice further exploration;
Have courage when faced with adversity
and a touch of improvisation;

A willingness to adapt or change; fun in planning, innovation;
Take comfort in your safe retreat - therein lies ones salvation.

Never be complacent for there will always be
Room for some improvement - toward perfect harmony.

And when your garden is in full bloom,
what is so important to do -
Is to take the time together to enjoy the 'love' you grew.

We spent ages choosing music and Dick played the fool, practising the ten paces it would take for me to reach him in the Shakespeare Room, where both the ceremony and wedding breakfast would be held. We chose 'You Say it Best When You Say Nothing At All' by Boyzone (or should I say Dick actually chose that one - I cannot for the life of me think why!) for when the guests were gathering; then 'Everything I Do' by Bryan Adams for my grand, but short entrance and that enchanting instrumental piece 'Canon' by Pachelbel for when signing the register.

Mum and my friend Cheryl came with me in search of a wedding dress. It didn't take long. The third dress I tried on was mine - exactly what I had in mind and it suited me perfectly. The jewellery they displayed on me with the dress became mine also.

I didn't get to see my flowers or cake until the day we arrived at the hotel. The Hotel was so excellent in its organisation of the finer details that the florist and cake-maker were in co-ordination with each other.

Arriving at Castle Combe the day before the wedding, we had a meal in the White Hart pub in the village, where we found the landlord to be a joker and very hospitable. As there were only twelve of us we were all part of everything, unlike some larger weddings where you barely get chance to speak to half the guests. The banter flowed all evening and Dick started talking with his hands - a sure sign he had had enough to drink. Actually, Dick always talked with his hands - it was one of his little mannerisms, but it was the accompanying glint in his eye that spelled trouble!

Then came those dreaded words from Paddy Flavin, Dick's best mate - "I'll walk you back Dick - we'll just have one for the road". Well I thought I wouldn't see him the next day if that happened - put those two together and one for the road becomes ten for the ditch! Thankfully, Paddy's wife, my friend, Cheryl, came to the rescue - "Don't worry Lin, they can have one for the road but I'll go with them". Phew what a relief! Why worry? I later heard a coke, two coffees and a Cointreau came to £25 - they sobered up very quickly and one for the road was literally that!

Having been serenaded by my dad in 'blackbird' form that morning I knew all was well with the world. I couldn't have wiped the smile off my face all day if I had wanted to. I did, however, wish dad could have been with me in person, as well as Dick's dad and brother John - Senior and Junior. We missed them all that day.

The photographer was a real hoot, a South African with a wicked sense of humour. Dick hates being photographed with a vengeance - in truth, so do I - but today was the exception and for me, my wedding pictures are the only really good set of photos I have ever had taken. The grounds of The Manor House are a fantastic backdrop with the river and bridges, the ornate Italian gardens, lovely architecture and the rooftops of the Manor House Hotel to give pictures that extra quality. While our guests enjoyed the Pimms, Dick was getting right browned off by all this malarkey with the cameraman. He had to laugh though when our snap-happy friend came out with the line "On a scale of one to ten - I'd give her one mate!" Tut tut! Finally the film ran out and we were free to share the Pimms and wait for Shakespeare room to be converted from ceremony to dining room - it was all so professionally achieved with the minimum of fuss.

It was a weird, but wonderful feeling - I became a wife, daughter-in-law, step-mum, step-aunt and sister-in-law all in one day - little wonder it was exhausting!

Having had a sumptuous, expertly served meal, followed by a rest, we all ventured out again late afternoon. I, of course kept my dress on all day - well the village is so perfect and quiet that it simply lends itself to such things. I walked about happily in my refinery determined to savour every moment to be the 'princess' in this fairytale village. We went back into the White Lion - where the landlord's first words were "Are you wearing that dress for a bet?" He laid on snacks for us and after a great evening we collapsed into bed, knowing a good day had been had by all.

Our guests stayed in the beautiful Mews cottages - each one varied by design with the homely touch of a different teddy-bear gracing the beds. I had stayed with mum in one of the cottages the night before the wedding - but tonight I had the pleasure of sharing the suite, 'Crew's Croft', with my husband. The room had a four poster bed, sherry decanter instead of coffee, a grandiose washing area with marble sinks and a separate bathroom. What more could I want? Nothing - absolutely nothing.

Castle Combe itself is steeped in history and I will summarise this for anyone wanting a taste of this little gem.

Our first ever trip to see what is described as 'the prettiest village in England' was from the direction of Bath on the A420 driving through dense lush woodland. As we approached the ancient Cumbe (a Saxon word, meaning valley) it was like an oyster shell opening to reveal a pearl - and so my love affair with Castle Combe began.

As you reach the old stone clapper bridge, known as the Roman bridge, over the River Bybrook, the honey-coloured Cotswold stone buildings and cottages unfold, unravaged by time. The wonky roof lines and irregular facades of the properties combined with the sweet scent of wood-burning fires make for a welcome like none other.

The streets are still narrow and winding - the only sign of the times are yellow lines and signposts on the roads. No television aerials or street lamps blight the scene. Castle Combe weaves its magic on you as you wander the paths gazing in awe at such 'quintessential' beauty. I find peace and inner calm with every step.

If you stand by the 14th Century Market Cross, the centrepiece of the village, and close your eyes you can almost hear the preaching friars addressing the crowds in the 15th century. The stone 'butter cross' nearby was used as a mounting block for horse riders and the water pump served the village well.

In Saxon times the village was divided into the Ober Combe (Upper) and Neider Combe (Under). The Upper Combe was mainly agricultural land, which was later used for training by the RAF in wartime and now houses the Castle Combe Circuit for car racing. A small industrial estate is sited on the grounds of the old dairy. Neither is evident from the centre of the village and thus nothing disturbs its harmony.

It is hard to picture now, but Castle Combe flourished as a major woollen cloth industry in the 15th century - the fast flowing Bybrook being instrumental in driving the mills. A Domesday survey in 1085 recorded two mills and in 1340 four corn mills and one fulling mill were shown. By the end of the 15th century thirteen mills operated in the valley. The woollen industry continued until the early 18th century, when the water level of the river dropped and there was insufficient power to operate the mills.

In 1440 there were weekly markets and a much celebrated three-day annual sheep fair, granted by the King on the feast of St George.

Human activity in the vicinity of the village is ancient. Lugbury Long Barrow dating from 2,500 BC is within a mile and in 1821 a skeleton of an 'ancient Briton' with primitive spear were unearthed. There is evidence of a pagan temple from 3 BC on the site of the existing St Andrews Church, which itself is referred to in historic documents of 1291, with rectors recorded from 1306. A Roman settlement in 43AD existed in the centre of the village and the Roman road, Fosseway, forms the western boundary of the parish.

A motte and bailey fortress was built to the north west of the village in 1140 AD but was abandoned in the 14th century in favour of a manor hall that had been built in the village.

Most of the Manor House was demolished in 18th century, then renovated and improved between 1876 and 1916. It was sold along with most of the village properties in 1947 and is now the exclusive Manor House Hotel with a golf course. The mews cottages in West Street are owned by the hotel and available as accommodation. The grounds are extensive and merit their own exploration. The romantic Italian gardens on the rise of the hill behind afford amazing views across the gabled roof and chimneys of The Manor House.

In the morning expect to see waiters in tail coats and waitresses in black and white Victorian style garb, walking to the mews cottages to serve breakfast to those who wish to tarry a while before starting their day.

The service and assistance offered in planning wedding services at the Manor House is exemplary. The advice and guidance is first class, yet unobtrusive, allowing you total freedom to have the day of your dreams. There is a luxurious elegance in the way they do business here - I was both smitten and awestruck - my cherished memories keep the smile upon my face, with tingling warmth to ward off the coldest of winters. I feel as intrinsically married to Castle Combe as I am to my husband.

The village has its own museum towards the Upper section of the village, and a car park away from the Lower village centre keeps the streets clear of tourist traffic.

Most of the buildings have their own story to tell, such as: the Dower House; the old Rectory; the old Bakery; the old Post Office; the Court House and the Weaver's House. Cottages retain old beams and original features. For the past five-hundred years the buildings have not altered.

In the 18th century there were ten ale houses in the parish. Today there is just The White Hart which has sold ale continuously for five-hundred years, and The Castle, which is also a hotel. The Castle was formerly known as The Salutation at the Cross - it was a popular hostelry with the monks on pilgrimage to Malmesbury.

The village cock pit was once in the rear yard of the neighbouring house (which was formerly The George). Castle Combe was used for the filming of Dr Dolittle in 1966.

In addition to a War memorial, alongside the river is a bench dedicated to the marriage of the Prince of Wales and Princess Diana. How poignant it was, when first showing our mothers the village that they paused for a rest on this very bench - it was the day of Diana's funeral!

As well as being a delightful historic path to tread, Castle Combe is only twelve miles from the majestic Roman city of Bath, offering a plethora of activities for any tourist.

There are walking trails in abundance around the village - including the circular Colham organic farm trail which starts and ends near the village centre. Being on the edge of the Cotswolds and bucolic Wiltshire you are never far from activity or simple repose. For a real piece of 'old England' this makes a wonderful weekend retreat and a 'must see' place in anyone's itinerary. For a wedding - it is perfect - just perfect.

Of course - a wedding is in essence just one special day with your loved one. Likewise, holidays are fun and carefree. For Dick and I, like everyone else - the rigours of daily life and the banal chores are far less glamorous. Compatibility here is much more important and Dick and I sang from the same song sheet in every aspect of life. 'Bunny', as I nicknamed him, became my life. He in turn called me 'Plum' which later, as I put on a bit of weight, turned affectionately to 'Plum-p'.

Don't get me wrong – there were occasions when we tried each others patience - he would drive me mad with his untidiness or 'manyana' attitude and I would infuriate him by needing to do everything immediately.

Dick's snoring was legendary – I have never heard anyone snore louder in my life – it was a shrewd move to be asleep before he came to bed to stand any chance of getting some sleep myself. Neither of us was perfect, nor always in total agreement, but we always had a willingness to work together and pull together. We never left the house without a goodbye kiss, nor slept on an argument. In truth arguments were few and far between - and never anything significant. Dick was impossibly hard to argue with - his calm and placid nature did not allow such things to manifest or fester. I was more highly strung - got frustrated faster, but like dad, I slid down the walls as quickly as climbing up them.

Dick hated the commercial hype of Christmas - and while I agree with him about the 'money-spinners' abounding at that time of year - I, for one, love Christmas. It has, and always will be for me, a time when families come together to enjoy and appreciate each others company. Dick and I used to add little clues for each other on our gift tags, but gave that up as trying to guess the contents meant it took so long to open them!

As much as Dick might bemoan Christmas festivities, and groan when I came home from shopping with yet another decoration - he did admire the room when it was bedecked with seasonal cheer.

Since dad died mum has always stayed with us from Christmas Eve until Boxing Day and I just love to see her eyes shining as she descends the stairs in the half-light of morning, when our two trees are ablaze with colour. It is a special moment for us both and one in which I always think of my dad.

I became Dick's secretary at both work, play and for charity business. He had been bought a computer as one of his leaving gifts from the police force and, believe me, he was not remotely computer literate at this time. I taught him to play cards, so that he could acquaint himself with using the mouse and we took it from there. He progressed very well, becoming e-mail and internet friendly, although I always had to check his documents for errors. He used spreadsheets for his investigative work, and formatting Microsoft Exel, even for me was tricky. It was the first time I saw him ever really lose his cool!

One day he came stomping downstairs in a right old 'tizzy' needing my help - not a happy bunny! His problem - well he was typing text but it wouldn't appear within the cell he'd typed it. After a long, hard look I discovered he had somehow managed to change the text colour from black to white - thus against a white background it was invisible. Fighting the desire to laugh I said to him "No amount of carrots is going to help you see that!"

Life was full of funny incidents - like the time, when staying with friends in France in their massive converted farmhouse, that Dick excelled himself as 'bat scarer'! We were given the second bedroom, which was absolutely huge, with windows front and back. The house is in a rural location, surrounded by rolling hills, fields and trees. Just before lights out one evening, Dick decided to measure the bedroom by pacing it out. He had just set about the task, when a bat flew in the window. As it began circling the room I screamed, pulling the sheets over my head. I then thought to turn the light up fully so I could at least see the beast properly - it was a big one and came perilously close to me as it performed its circuits of the boudoir.

Sir Galahad told me not to worry, that he'd chase it out of the opposite window. I was then treated to fifteen minutes of Dick flapping his arms, chasing a bat and wearing nought but his underpants. I was apoplectic with laughter. Dick finally succeeded in his mission and we closed the curtains to prevent a repeat performance. Thankfully the walls of the house are so thick, David and Jan heard nothing of the shenanigans!

There are so many amusing anecdotes I could tell, but my favourite has to be one night, three days before our holiday to Thailand. I was woken by torchlight outside at 3 a.m. I elbowed Dick in the ribs trying to rouse him from his snoring slumber.

I then saw the light shining through the front door. "Dick, Dick - there's someone at the door - I'm going - you'd better follow me". With a sharp jab in his rib-cage I dashed to the door, to find a policewoman on the step. A motorist had just demolished our front wall - having fallen asleep at the wheel he failed to negotiate the bend - thankfully he wasn't badly hurt.

As I stood in the kitchen with the officer, so Dick appeared - a 'vision in lilac.' I had, in my haste, pulled his robe off the door, leaving him with mine. Trying to stifle a fit of the giggles I said "Cross dressing tonight are we darling?" Unfortunately the police woman had no sense of humour - ho hum - well it was night shift I guess!

Having fun has been our byword, although there have been tougher times, like in 2004 when Dick became seriously ill with diverticulitis. An abscess had formed in his large intestine, forcing a gap between the bowel and bladder through which tiny particles of faeces were being passed into his urinary tract. It was excruciatingly painful for him and for a while we thought he had kidney stones. We were both incredibly relieved when the colonoscopy identified the problem. I had been terrified he had bowel cancer, so this alternative, no matter how nasty, was preferable. That said, Dick had to have a sigmoid colectomy, which is major surgery, to remove the damaged section of bowel, and was hospitalised for two weeks.

Working on the principle that most men are acutely embarrassed by all things 'cuddly', I tried to hurry his release process along by taking in a small cuddly toy every day – each one bearing its own message tag for Dick. I thought he would make haste to get out as soon as possible – as it happened the whole entourage were lined up on the window sill before he was discharged. His recovery took three months but at least he was home before Christmas. The decorations went up earlier than normal in honour of his homecoming.

Dick craved another cruise and had been hoping we would do one in the Far East, near Thailand that winter. The operation ruled this out, in any case I refused to go anywhere without good medical facilities, hence why we chose the two back-to back cruises for October of the following year, when he would be back to full health. As it turned out, the shocking tsunami struck in just the areas he had wanted to visit - lady luck, at least for now, had been shining on us.

We did go back to the Red Sea, to Sharks Bay for a quick week the following February - it was a wonderfully relaxing time. Having left the man-made beach for the afternoon we would sit at an elevated bar, just watching the sun shimmering across the sea as its heat began to wane. It was wholly therapeutic and I could have sat there mesmerised all day.

We were both looking forward to our plans for moving house - we wanted to go to the Cotswolds - no more than ninety minutes by road from the Watford area - allowing for reasonable access to both our mothers. Bricket Wood, for us, had become a rat run with declining services. It is a commuter belt area and, while having easy access to major arterial routes, the roads enveloping us are noisy, fast and jammed solid with vehicles. It would be a pleasure to find a real village, where the song of the birds no longer had to compete with traffic. This venture took us on many short trips to the Cotswolds and with pen poised we would mark down good potential areas. Thinking ahead to our dotage, we covered everything from bus routes, local shops, a village pub, access to trains and doctors etc.

We wanted it to be a move we would only need to do once - so it had to be the right one. It was great fun and we found some little gems. I started a spreadsheet so we could look at properties on the internet - and named it 'Location, Location, Location' after the television series. Somehow, in spite of our fun, I always felt it was a pipe dream - I was not wrong.

One of Dick's favourite phrases has always been "No matter how much wrong someone does you, you don't attack their soul - everyone has a soul". If I heard him say that to people once, I must have heard it a thousand times. It is quite lovely and he of course, is so right. Many people may upset you, be thoughtless or unkind, often unintentionally or not realising they have done so. It is no excuse to be 'nasty' back.

Unfortunately, there have been times when people have been like that to Dick, and then I find it hard to bite my tongue. Although Dick was not a church-goer, he was the most Christian man I have ever known, in the way he lived his life and touched the lives of all who met him. He would not push himself forward or seek attention - but sometimes, especially where his health was concerned he should have done so. It was at such times that he needed me - his little 'Rottweiler' by his side - if he wasn't going to fight for himself - I sure as heck would do it for him.

Dick after his glider flight   Chauffeur-driven to the theatre

Steven, me, Neil & Dick   Peggy & John   'The Two Mums'

Garden shots

At the Amber Fort, India   Golfing in USA

Somewhere Over the Rainbow

Guadalest - Spain

Chance meeting - with Bill & Mary in New Zealand

Parascending in New Zealand

Castle Combe village centre

A marriage made in heaven

CHAPTER 11

RAINBOW'S END

'God grant me serenity to accept what I cannot change, courage to change the things that I can, and wisdom to know the difference'.

Reinhold Niebuhr

These last two Chapters were not supposed to exist. There was to be no end to the rainbow - the pot of gold was to continue happily ever after. Life is not always like that and as we found, it can deal a cruel blow when you are least expecting it.

In the summer of 2006 Dick started suffering from sporadic sickness after consuming food. It was nothing too sinister to start with, but enough to merit a doctors appointment. Blood tests were all clear so an appointment was sought for an endoscopy examination. During this six-week-long wait his sickness became more frequent and caused us a great deal of anxiety. Some understatement - I was terrified. I dared not ponder too long on what may be wrong - nevertheless, in my heart, even then, I felt the distant rumble of thunder and a sense of foreboding. Dick has never had a brilliant appetite, and apart from a good breakfast, he never craved food like I did.

Any stress or anxiety would invariably manifest itself in his digestive system and he admitted this had always been so. He definitely had a weak digestive tract and I feel the diverticulitis had been evidence of this.

A little brightness did arrive in our lives at this time - in the form of Tristan our adorable little grandson, born to Dick's son Neil and his girlfriend, Sara. Tristan was a source of pure delight to Dick - he was smitten at first sight and thrilled to be a grandad. As I watched him holding this little bundle, my heart turned flip-flops, praying to God this little baby would grow up to know and love this very special man - his amazing grandad. Dick would be everyone's idea of a perfect grandad - he would be patient, funny, encouraging, a source of inspiration and the best possible counsellor for a child heading towards adulthood.

In the autumn, Dick was pleased as punch when he was offered the job of Operations Manager for Outforce, but, worried about his health he nearly turned it down. The job was to be held over until he was better so there was no need for Dick to fret.

We had some building work done at home at the beginning of October. To escape the mess we went away for a week to Suffolk - it wasn't a good week. Dick was eating little more than tiny starter portions and he was losing weight with increasing momentum. For a man who was slender and 6'2" tall, his weight at its very best was twelve and a half stone, but he was shedding it fast.

After the diverticulitis operation he dropped down to ten stone, which was understandable, but he had gradually built back up to his optimum weight.

On returning from the trip the endoscopy appointment awaited us on the doormat - it was in two days time - the 10th October. The test was performed and it was not good news - although unconfirmed it appeared Dick had an oesophageal tumour - which after biopsy results and endless different consultation appointments was confirmed. Dick had cancer. This time there were no alternative illnesses - our worse fears were realised and our world literally *rocked*.

Dick had an adenocarcinoma of the oesophagus (this is the type usually caused through acid reflux). The tumour was in the lower part of the oesophagus near the neck of the stomach - an awkward position. It was described as being poorly differentiated, which meant it was aggressive, but should respond better to chemotherapy. There was no spread - it was potentially operable. Had there been any evident spread - or metastasis - to other organs then it would have been inoperable and the prognosis poor.

The plan was for Dick to have three, three-weekly cycles of chemotherapy with a view to shrinking the tumour, followed by a major operation to remove it. The cycle would begin with chemotherapy administered intravenously at Mount Vernon hospital over twenty-four hours, backed up by oral chemo tablets to take until the next cycle commenced. While the chances of re-occurrence were quite high I thought at the very least it would buy us a few more years together.

Soon after the diagnosis was confirmed, Dick and I spent a difficult, emotional day making plans for a funeral that we prayed would never happen. It was hard to broach this subject at all. I told Dick that I felt 'we needed to have a talk' and intuitively knowing what I meant he said "Don't you think I know I need to review my music?" On our Saturday evening chats as we played music we had often joked "Play this one for me at my funeral".

It wasn't that we thought Dick was going to die imminently - we didn't, but cancer poses sufficient risk that you are wise to be prepared. It is an unknown quantity, sometimes with a mind of its own in spite of the assault on it from toxic drugs or radiotherapy.

People have since asked me how on earth we managed it - how could we be that strong? The short answer is that we took every other decision in life together - so why would we not do this - such an important issue could not be ignored. We agreed it was to be a conversation we would have once only, and once done we wouldn't revisit it.

We spent the best part of a wretched Sunday in the conservatory making notes, which I transferred to the computer. There were some lighter moments - like when I asked what type of coffin he would want. He replied "Cardboard" - okay if you're having a 'green burial' but as we weren't I responded with "Over *my* dead body". We also went through everything we needed to do to get our house in order.

Choosing music was the most difficult task. Dick hears only the melody, whereas I always hear the lyrics first. We played so many tracks, me repeating the lyrics to Dick as we went, to find suitable material, not commonly used. Dick mused over "Bat Out of Hell" but I put my foot down "Think of your mother!" "Okay how about 'Heaven Can Wait' then?" One of my looks told him all he needed to know! Joking aside, importantly Dick wanted every song to hold a message - for me, family, friends or colleagues - he was incredibly thoughtful - it was so typical of Dick.

We chose six tracks in all - and I have to confess to breaking my heart when we decided 'Everything I Do' by Bryan Adams had to be included, as it had been at our wedding. 'Bring You Home' by Ronan Keating was another track with fantastic words conveying the message that you are not alone, and 'Friends' by The Osmonds - which, for Dick as a peace-maker - was a fitting plea for all to be friends. Yes - he really did choose an Osmonds track, which my brother said just proved he really was unwell! Everyone could still have their little piece of him - even if it were in death!

Dick had a CT scan on 17th October and the new PET scan on 6th November - this is sophisticated technology, and Mount Vernon has one of only five PET scanners in the country. They still showed no metastasis to our huge relief. It transpires that that neither scanning method is without deficiencies. We had to wait some time before chemotherapy could commence - beds at Mount Vernon are like gold dust.

The tenuous thread we were dangling by and the patience of Dr Harrison, the chemotherapy consultant was wearing thin.

Dick was now almost unable to eat anything solid - instead I was getting prescribed nutritional support drinks from the pharmacists and getting as much soup and slop into him as he could tolerate. Surprisingly he could still eat mars and cereal bars, so I stocked up with as many different goodies and treats for him as I could. It is one such circumstance in which you can eat as much trash as possible - calories, no matter how hollow, are requisite.

For weeks now I had been unable to sleep past four or five in the morning. I would go upstairs to sit on the computer and rid myself of anxiety. I needed to keep my positive force for Dick in his waking hours. I can only imagine what he was privately going through, but like me he was cheerful, positive and upbeat on the surface. This attitude was vital and we were determined to get things moving. The frustration of waiting so long took its toll on us both, and our nerves were getting frayed, yet still we tried to quash any negativity. I recall an occasion when Dick was wandering about the patio in his bathrobe - it started raining, so I yelled at him to come inside. "You'll catch your death of cold!" I said. We both looked at each other and burst out laughing at the idiocy of that well-used phrase at such a time.

The rumble of thunder in my heart was increasing in its intensity with forked lightning thrown in - I was petrified. While Dick's mental approach was, as always, magnificent, I seriously worried about his constitution - which was far from robust. Had the cancer been anywhere else he it might have been easier - but being unable to eat meant his body mass suffered - and this too is essential with any cancer treatment, hence the need for any calorific intake.

By 4th December Dick's weight was down to ten stone, three pounds - he was starting to have problems keeping fluids down and losing a pound a day in weight. I spoke to our wonderful Macmillan nurse, Caroline and expressed my growing consternation. We had a bed confirmed for chemotherapy to commence on 12th December.

By 6th December Dick was down to ten stone and being sick at night as well as during the daytime. I could see he was getting badly dehydrated. I spoke with Caroline, then Dr Harrison's secretary and was instructed to take Dick to the Accident and Emergency Department at Hemel Hempstead hospital. Saline drips, and later drip feeds were administered to maintain Dick's fluid intake and nutritional support levels. He was, at least fit to commence chemotherapy as planned. After treatment at Mount Vernon it was back to Hemel hospital - still unable to eat or drink, the sickness continued.

There were no apparent side effects from the chemo, which we were told could start to shrink the tumour within a couple of days and so enable him to take on board more nutrition.

We were armed with a cocktail of tablets - two strengths of capecitabine (oral chemo) as well as tablets for anti-sickness, anti-diarrhoea and anti-constipation. I had to pay attention to the nurse who instructed on what to take when and how. Dick was mentally overloaded by the treatment itself. The chemo didn't start to shrink the tumour - Dick wasn't conforming to the norm. With the continuation of sickness the oral chemo tablets were rendered ineffective as they weren't staying inside his body long enough to begin working. Pumps of anti-sickness drugs were attached to his stomach in an attempt to stem the sickness. For a time they seemed to help a little, but insufficiently to significantly improve the situation.

Later it was decided a stent should be fitted - this would force a gap past the tumour thus allowing food and drink to be ingested normally. This operation was done on 21st December. It was expected that it would take a couple of days for the stomach to settle as the fitting of a stent - especially at the neck of the stomach entrance would rough Dick's insides up.

I was spitting feathers the day after this operation - I arrived to find five bowls of vomit on his bedside table - they had been there since the night. It took me two seconds to dispose of them and then I went to find a nurse, and promptly ripped her head off about the lack of care and health hazards.

There were other instances when I was less than impressed - such as it taking two hours before they replaced his saline and nutritional drips. I was furious and just wished I could have him home with me, where he would have my constant attention. He did at least get moved nearer to the nurses' station later and was better tended to for a time.

After several days without any signs of improvement whatsoever we knew the stent was not working. Another CT scan was done, and the consultant wasn't happy with the look of his stomach lining - there also appeared to be a blockage in the small intestine.

On Christmas Eve the doctor allowed Dick to come home for twenty-four hours - with stomach pumps attached to try to stem his sickness. In reality he was far too ill to be home, although I was glad that he could sit once more in his favourite armchair, away from the hospital. As it was he slept or was sick almost continually, save for an hour or so when his sons, Sara and Tristan came to visit us. I can still see Dick reaching out to the baby and not having the strength to hold him - it was painful to watch, and cuts like a knife now - it was the last time he saw his beloved grandson.

That night Dick couldn't sleep in bed, despite the pillows being arranged to suit his needs - he worried about disturbing me and returned to the armchair at 1 a.m. I couldn't have been more disturbed by the sight of this precious, vital man, so perilously ill.

At one point on Christmas morning, he walked into the kitchen as I was preparing myself some lunch - I almost didn't recognise him. His face was haunted, hollow - a walking ghost. It was all I could do to stop myself from gasping out loud. I have never felt such all-encompassing fear.

Returning to hospital on Christmas Day was totally heart-wrenching. Dick thought he would come home again, but at one look at my face he said "You don't think I should come out again do you?" Of *course* I wanted him home, but the reality is that he was far too ill. He needed to be fit enough for the next course of chemo on 2nd January and two days of absolutely no fluids or nutrition were going to seriously jeopardise that. So, on the ward he told them he needed to stay. For the first time I broke my heart in front of him - I am cross with myself for doing so, but simply couldn't help it.

I so desperately wanted him with me - now - always, but knew I could not give him the medical help he required - if the drips could have been administered at home I would have not let him return to hospital - not ever. It cuts me to the quick feeling as if I had made this decision - but we had to look ahead at what was to come, and the importance of us getting through this for Dick's survival. In hindsight I would have done, oh, so much differently - but we aren't blessed with the powers of foresight, and do all that is humanly possible, borne out of love.

On Boxing Day I sat with him for almost eight hours - he was only fully awake for twenty minutes of that time, save for reading the newspaper a while and being sick. It was draining on my resources and my heart was in tatters by the time I left for the day.

Dick's veins were getting harder to find, and the needles kept painfully missing, so a central line was fitted to his neck to enable easy administration of the nutritional support. I should say that these drip feeds only keep you alive, they contain one thousand, five-hundred calories - they won't increase your weight, but at least give you the vital minerals and vitamins. Dick at this point was just over nine stone.

Dick's morale plummeted heavily after Christmas, and desperate to find a way to lift his spirits, I wrote him a letter, leaving it with him to ponder over:

28th December 2006
My Darling Dick,
I know you are finding things a struggle right now and that it is hard to keep a positive frame of mind - that's okay - you are allowed to have moments like this. You aren't feeling sorry for yourself; you are just having an almighty inner battle.

Don't be so hard on yourself - take a few deep, slow breaths and tell yourself it will be okay. Treat this cancer like a top ten target criminal - now that's a fight you could never resist - and a battle you seldom lost - this will be no different.

On days of weakness, draw on my strength - lean on me - I will not fail you.

You are the most wonderful man I've ever known - the only person who truly puts everyone and everything before himself. You have the greatest capacity for loving others - the most generous spirited man I have ever known. I love you more than words can ever say. How blessed was the day that I found you - my irreplaceable special love. Our love sustains us at this difficult time and I cherish it with all my heart.

On days of weakness, picture our wedding day, my dream come true - and know you made all that possible. Think of all the fantastic adventures we have taken and all the ones you still want to take - we will do them. Think of our weekends away - the beautiful hotels, quiet corners and pretty villages - which ones do you wish to return to? Make a list and we will start at the top and work down.

Look ahead to next year when we will take the two mums away for their Christmas treat, and to our little Tristan turning from a baby into a toddler.

Look to the joy that lies ahead for you once this battle has been won - focus on what you want to achieve in your life and on us growing old together. Look into my eyes and know that I will do all in my power for you, look into my heart and see that love has a strength that can conquer all.

We may both have moments of weakness - but together we are strong - always.

I love you darling,
Forever yours, Lin xxx

The following day, Dick wasn't sick at all. The day after that he had started writing his list of places he wanted to visit - he was slightly sick but certainly much improved. I felt we were making headway. The letter, at least, appeared to have given him his fighting spirit back - the sickness, however, returned.

On 2nd January 2007 the second course of chemo took place at Mount Vernon. This went okay, save for side effects of diarrhoea, which to Dick was the gravest indignity. I had such compassion and sympathy for him - he was a private, deeply sensitive man, and was acutely embarrassed by what was happening to him. His hair, cropped as it was, was also starting to come out as we knew it would.

After chemo was complete, we were waiting to return him to Hemel hospital as planned. It took ages to see Dr Harrison, and when we did we were told he would instead be going to Watford hospital.

The blockage in his intestine appeared to be the cause of the fluids being rejected - the plan was to operate to bypass this blockage and to enable us to get back on track. It was an arduous day - and the third different hospital Dick was to call home within three days.

An injection - referred to by Dr Harrison as 'the golden shot' was administered to bring his blood cells up to an acceptable level to facilitate the operation. His body would not endure it without this treatment. It is incredibly expensive stuff, so I knew they were optimistic about its success.

The staff at Watford hospital were very efficient and kind and Dick was certainly happier there than at Hemel - facially he looked pretty good. The operation was to be on Monday 8th January - he was counting the days.

During the weekend before the operation I noticed that his vomit was more like pure blood with a little saliva mixed in. I pointed this out to the nursing staff, who were already monitoring it. It really worried me - this looked different - and over the months I had become an expert at seeing changes in his regurgitated fluid - I had after all had plenty of practice by now.

Monday finally arrived and Dick was taken away for his operation at 10 a.m. I had hoped to speak to him beforehand, but missed him by minutes. I had lunch with my dear friend, Val, while waiting to phone the hospital. I had given her an onerous task and she was a real brick. We stood together in the car park as I made the call, and sobbed in each others arms with sheer relief to hear that Dick was on his way back to the ward - I had expected him to be in intensive care at best.

I went to see him straight away, although naturally he was still asleep, and as always after an operation, looked shocking. I was not too disturbed by this as he had looked the same after the diverticulitis operation and I knew what to expect. He came round some time after I got there, but I didn't stay long as he needed rest and recovery. It was agonising to see him lying there, so vulnerable and helpless - so unlike the Dick I knew and loved. I took a few breaks, then left him to sleep and came home.

The following day disturbed me far more. Dick looked almost as bad as when he returned from the operation. The oxygen mask was still in situ and he was wired up for sound - I could barely get close to him for all the tubes, monitors and machines. Dick awoke when I arrived, to tell me he had seen the surgeon, Dr Livingstone - that the operation was a success - but he didn't know any more. He asked if I had seen anyone yet? Hardly - I'd just walked in. I told him I would be seeing a junior doctor soon. Dick went straight back to sleep.

When I saw the doctor he couldn't tell me much - yes, they had done the operation, but it wasn't quite as they'd hoped, and the blockage in the small intestine appeared to be another tumour. I would have to see Dr Livingstone or one of the operating team for proper medical information. What was I to do with that news? I needed firm facts before talking to Dick, who at this stage wasn't well enough to receive such unsubstantiated information.

When I went back to Dick, he opened his eyes - amazing how he could come round when he needed to! Looking squarely into his eyes I told him I only knew the same as him, the junior doctor wasn't much help and I needed to speak to the operating team. I prayed he would believe that, but knowing how intuitive Dick was, I doubted it. I loathed holding back on him but had no choice. When I had real facts then I could be totally honest with him - I had far too much respect for Dick than to be anything else.

Again I couldn't stay too long that day - in desperate need of rest Dick waved me away several times. Reluctantly I left, as always saying how much I loved him. I read him a card I had found especially for him. It said 'Love isn't the person you can see yourself with; it's the person you can't see yourself without' - never a truer word spoken.

As I was leaving the ward I remembered I'd left cards and things to take home. I returned to Dick's bedside, only to catch what appeared to be a tear trickling from the corner of his eye. It could have been the oxygen making his eyes water - I don't know - but my instincts told me it was a tear. Did he know more than I?

I left the hospital with the heaviest heart in the world. I knew this illness was going against us. I typed out a list of questions for the surgical team - only when they were answered would I know the way forward.

That evening I decided to go and see Paddy and Cheryl and spent three hours with them discussing Dick's situation. I knew that Dick wanted Paddy to deliver an address at his funeral, should he die. I now truly feared I was going to lose this wonderful man - the mainstay of my life. We talked about all the possible scenarios - save for one.

At 9 a.m. the next morning, while working at a client's house, so my mobile phone rang. The call was a carbon copy of that which my mum took the day my father died. "Could you come to the hospital please - your husband isn't so well this morning". I felt as if I'd just been garrotted – my stomach lurched so hard I thought it would rise up to choke me.

I left work at haste, using every ounce of inner reserve to concentrate on the road - not to panic - to just simply get there safely. The traffic was heavy, the rain belted down - and here I was with a forty-minute drive to get to my husband. I thought I had probably already lost him, but prayed against all hope that he was still with me.

I abandoned the car, went hell for leather to the ward and was ushered straight into a side room. Dick was alive, but he was dying. The surgical team were all there to answer my questions but the only thing I needed right then was to be with my husband. I was shaking uncontrollably. *No!* This could not be happening - not to us!

When I went into Dick a nurse sat holding his hand, a sweet touch. He was still on oxygen, his lungs going through the motions - but not much else. All other machines had been removed. His eyes had rolled back and his corneas were drying. Quite frankly he already looked dead - his appearance was so dreadful.

I got on the bed and held him; talked to him - prayed like mad he could hear me. The nurse allowed me to remove his mask to give him a kiss. His mouth was so cold, but his hands were warm. With the mask back in place I didn't stop talking, thanking him and loving him as I waited for my life to crumble - tears coursing down my face. A nurse finally separated him from the oxygen mask and within a minute, my beloved Dick left the comfort of my arms and moved on.

The utter devastation I felt cannot be explained in words - it was total. In truth my Dick never really returned from that operation. A nurse helped me remove Dick's wedding ring - it went straight onto my hand and I clutched it for all I was worth.

In the side room I called Paddy, who thankfully worked at Watford Football Club next door. He arrived and we stood sobbing helplessly in each other's arms. He had lost his best friend, I had lost my 'one true love' - my life could never be the same again. My 'Bunny' was gone.

I hear people say about their loved ones looking peaceful when they passed away. I didn't feel there was anything peaceful in Dick's death. He had been so ravaged by this terrible disease, all I could see was this person that didn't closely resemble my husband - the 'post-operative Dick' looked nothing like the man I knew and loved. The illness had taken him from me already. I could only pray he had moved into his coma without pain. Of course his, oh, so beautiful soul and spirit were not touched by the disease - they remained the same and I thanked heaven for that small mercy.

Paddy and I both had phone calls to make. Cheryl and another close friend, Mary arrived at the hospital to find me in a trance - shock had set in.

I had phoned Dick's brothers, Michael and David and my brother, Martin. Michael went to his mum, Peggy. Martin went to my mum - getting her to pack a bag so she could stay with me when I got home. Paddy phoned Steven and Neil - I was incapable by then.

The boys, Sara, Michael and Peggy came to the hospital to say their farewell to a beloved father, son and brother. Dear Peggy - she could only think of me. My heart broke for her - in losing a second son - her friend and counsellor - it was just three days before her ninety-second birthday. Paddy was immense for me that day; I could not have got through it without him or indeed all the support of my family and friends.

One of the worst jobs I had was to pack Dick's belongings into his holdall as his earthly body still lay on the bed. I felt like I was invading his space. I went in again for one final agonising farewell before leaving the ward and going home to a life that, at the time, felt devoid of all colour.

Back home everyone rallied. We sat there - our wedding party - save for Peggy who had returned home with friends. The brandy bottle was out and I certainly needed it – despite the fact I don't usually touch it as it gives me a bad head. Dave Perry, Dick's chosen vicar arrived later and we started activating those funeral plans that had come to fruition all too soon.

The shock at the speed with which things had happened was unbelievable. It transpired that Dick also had cancer of the stomach, which earlier scans had failed to detect, and the additional intestinal tumour. In short - cancer was the whole way through from the oesophagus to bowel. He didn't stand a chance.

Dick would have had a torrid time ahead of him, his cancer was inoperable and his life would have ended in severe pain. This I would wish on no-one, especially not this gentle, special man. Neither of us could have borne it and I am thankful that he has not had to endure any pain – he is safe from harm, nothing and nobody can ever hurt him again. The fact that I had been helpless to protect Dick and prevent his suffering was the hardest thing to bear. I was there for him always, as promised, yet, save for the love, support, encouragement and compassion I gave, I was totally powerless to stop the havoc this disease wreaked - this is what hurts most of all.

How did I feel? Bereft, absolutely lost, heart-broken and paddling in deep waters without any direction - I was in free-fall. Having mum at home with me over the next ten days or so was a godsend. She was simply wonderful and I could not have got through without her support, love and total understanding. But, like her, I knew I had to start as I meant to go on.

Registering Dick's death - seeing his name in black and white, was like a deep stab wound to the ribs - it was so final - a huge reality check.

As well as instigating the funeral plans there was much to do. I also had some thirty-five letters to write – the usual notifications. I decided to set myself a task each day – prioritising the letters, I would accomplish a few before mum got up each morning. I was getting next to no sleep, but I had at least got many things to focus on. This helped me build some structure into each day, instead of numbly drifting without purpose, waiting for the next tidal wave of grief to explode – and explode they did. When this happens it is like a sledgehammer crashing down on you, it takes my legs from beneath me, casting me into oblivion, until it finally subsides and calmness descends.

I remember the very first time the sledgehammer descended - it frightened me senseless! It was late at night and I suddenly was convulsed with this agonising wave of tears. They wracked my body and I could hardly breathe with the force at which they hit me. They just wouldn't stop - wave upon wave of heart-wrenching pain surged through me.

I found myself walking about the garden, in my dressing gown, clutching Sidney the seal, which Dick had bought me on our very first Christmas. I could hear myself calling to Dick "Where are you darling? Where are you?" Not only had I lost Dick but I truly thought I had lost my mind too. I phoned Rosie in America - knowing she would be up at this ungodly hour at least. We talked for ages and finally I felt myself calming down again. When the sledgehammer released me from its grip I felt weak, exhausted and so terribly sad. This whole attack had lasted several hours and had totally drained me. Gradually the sledgehammer attacks have become less severe - or at least have not lasted so long - but grief will out and you just have to let it take its course.

I couldn't unzip the holdall I'd brought home from the hospital for almost two weeks - it was like Pandora's Box - I was scared to open it for fear of the graphic images and pain that would leap out.

Mum and I set a day to deal with Dick's clothes and this holdall, then did so as speedily as possible. It was an acutely painful task. You feel guilty at disposing of such things, of emptying the cupboards - at the time you feel as if you are literally sweeping your loved one away. There is no way round it - it has to be done - it will always hurt as it is so personal - and needs to be done early on in the grieving process. Even now I come across little artefacts, paper with Dick's writing on it, and it gives me a jolt - but now I am starting take comfort from these reminders.

I spread my clothes about in the wardrobes, as empty space would be equally as painful as seeing Dick's clothes. I also took over Dick's favourite chair in the sitting room - making it my own. Thus, I would not be gazing at the empty chair and got to view the lounge from another aspect. Small moves maybe - but they made a huge difference to me.

Of course, not only had the worst thing happened to my life with Dick, so the rot continued. I didn't at first experience those 'nice' little touches that we got when dad died. Lady Luck seemed determined to keep smacking me in the face.

I discovered that the will company and storage group that held our wills had in fact not got our original signed documents.

The fact that I sent them recorded delivery and did a 'track and trace' some six years earlier counted for nothing - this far on, I could not prove loss of documents by the company and had to go through the rigours of probate. I engaged Dick's solicitor, a kind man, who had a calming influence on my delicate state of mind.

I had other problems with banks cancelling direct debits and debit cards in error, Dick's police pension being paid in full when it should have been cancelled – and several other issues like these, purely because recipients of my letters couldn't carry out instructions properly. It made it doubly stressful as I had to re-send many letters and chase people to do their jobs. Then the toaster kept overheating, the shower started leaking and the washing machine – and so it went on. The toaster and leaks somehow corrected themselves – maybe Dick was starting to help me out – just as well as I was at the limit of how much more I could take.

We had two weeks, two days to wait for the funeral. That may seem like an eternity to many, but in truth, I was glad of it – it enabled some of the numbness to wear off and allowed me to mentally prepare myself for the ordeal. I wanted to maintain my dignity and make Dick proud of me – I wasn't going to let him down. I decided he should be dressed in his favourite golf shirt and trousers. I took the clothes to the funeral directors, with firm instructions about the collar being out over the jumper – and the jumper pulled down at the back. These were two things I always straightened out for Dick when he got dressed! The golf shirt he wore provided a lighter moment some time after the funeral when Dick's brother, David, enquired after it - thinking it would be nice to have Dick's favourite golfing top. Steven had told him it might be a problem - indeed it was - we couldn't help but see the funny side of it!

I wrote a poem to go on the back of my funeral flowers card, which I had produced on the computer using my favourite wedding photograph. The poem wasn't my best work as it was forced instead of spontaneous, but it conveyed my feelings for the moment.

Although my heart is broken
I'll find strength in thoughts of you
The love we shared together
Will keep me pulling through;

I'm so proud of you my darling
In the way you lived your life,
For you touched the hearts of everyone -
I'm so honoured to be your wife.

You will walk with me forever
From dawn to dusk each day -
I'll see your smile and hear your laughter
With every step along the way.

How blessed I was to find you,
I thank the Lord above
For everything you mean to me -
My irreplaceable, one 'true love'.

Mum stayed with me for ten days before I sent her home to allow us both some rest. She returned on the eve of the funeral to stay for another couple of nights.

With the funeral beckoning I had to sort out my outfit. I had a lovely black shift cocktail dress and long black jacket that were a perfect match - Dick loved me in both so that was an easy choice for me to make. I wore my wedding jewellery and the florist made a beautiful fresh flower corsage to break up the 'black'. High heels were going to be a problem as I am not adept at standing in them for long - I am happier padding around in bare feet or flip-flops - but I had to be elegant on this day. My hairdresser did my hair beautifully and thus I was ready to bid my love farewell.

I purchased three slots at West Herts Crematorium – allowing ample time for the addresses and utilisation of all the music. I couldn't bear things to be rushed - wanting to take time to honour Dick's wishes fully. The drive up to the crematorium was astounding with a massive throng of some four-hundred people lining the way in. I knew there would be a healthy attendance, but even so it took my breath away.

The Hertfordshire Constabulary drape covered the coffin, with my cream lily spray on top. Another mark of respect was the police Guard of Honour. In truth Dick had only conceded to the drape, but I knew it was only his humility that prevented him agreeing to the 'guard', so I made just this one change to his wishes. I'm sure he will forgive me, knowing I did this to afford greater comfort to his mother and sons. I already knew how much respect he was held in within the police force – after all no-one respected him more than I, but after thirty-one years totally dedicated and highly effective service to the public and police force nobody deserved it more richly than he.

Dick's friends from the Friday Club and Outforce were pallbearers – faces like stone, drawn and grief-stricken. They had carried him with them in life therefore it was fitting that they take him to the end of the road.

As 'Everything I do' played out, so I walked in behind Dick, flanked by Steven and Neil – we were there to do their father proud, no matter how hard that song tugged at my inner core.

A favourite picture of Dick – both for me and his friends (taken on our last cruise) was blown up to life-size and rested against the coffin. A happy, healthy Dick, with glass of red wine held up as if to toast us all. The Dick I knew and loved. The photograph held me captive throughout the service - it is the image I strive to hold onto.

As the Ronan Keating track 'Bring You Home' played, I gazed at Dick, remembering us in the conservatory - such a beautiful song, with words that afford me great comfort and strength. As the service progressed I spoke to Dick – 'this is just how we planned it darling – you would be so pleased'. A friend told me that when The Osmonds track 'Friends' was playing, so the sun emerged from behind a cloud and illuminated half the room – she said it was stunning. It was another message well-delivered in that case.

For Dave Perry it was a job well done and Paddy, whose heart was breaking was simply wonderful. Steven also spoke on behalf of him and Neil, conveying their own personal message and using snippets from the one hundred and fifty cards and e-mails I had received following Dick's death. Dick would have been so proud of his sons on this day – they carried themselves so well with calm dignity.

We only had one sung hymn - *'Make Me a Channel of Your Peace'*. Again - it spoke volumes about Dick's character - it was another thought provoking message.

Baby Tristan continued his Grandad's tradition for liking a good sleep – he was in peaceful slumber throughout the service – blissfully unaware of the pain and loss in the hearts surrounding him.

The funeral concluded, as always, with the curtain call. I kissed the photograph of Dick as it was handed to me. We were ready to leave.

It was such a cold day, that, after the service we went without delay to the Metropolitan Police Sports and Social Club at Bushey, for the wake – or 'celebration of Dick's life'. With so many people at the funeral it would have been impossible to meet and greet all, especially with a baby and ninety-two year old in our midst. I was shaking uncontrollably – partly with the cold, but mainly from the strain of retaining some serenity and simply 'holding myself' together. I felt sad that I didn't get a chance to speak to everyone there, but the vast majority of them attended the wake so I had the opportunity to say thank you.

The wake was provided by Dick's Friday Club friends – a touching gesture for which I am so grateful. Dick would have loved the 'event' – it was so like the numerous police bashes we'd attended in the past – people swapping stories, the sound of laughter. This was no different, other than the purpose behind it, thus the utmost respect was also in evidence. It was something of a police reunion – with people present spanning well in excess of thirty years service.

For those outside the police 'club' it can be quite daunting, but I welcomed it – it was a safe and comfortable environment for me at such an awful time.

I got to experience first hand what it was like 'being Dick' that day, as it seemed everyone still wanted a piece of him – but this time through me. People had lovely stories to share and were tremendously supportive.

I had prepared a small address of my own. I owed it to Dick to speak on his behalf to all the wonderful people present who had meant so much to him. How I managed it I'm not sure but I was determined it must be done. The brandy flowed, warming me up and sustaining me all afternoon and evening. I wouldn't advocate anyone drinking double brandies for eight hours continuously, but with the adrenalin coursing through my system it didn't touch me – in spite of the fact I didn't eat anything – and the spread laid on looked magnificent.

I spoke clearly, and managed to stay on my heels the entire day – a first I am sure. It was nevertheless a long and shattering ordeal. The only kick back I felt was that of complete exhaustion the next morning – you can only keep up the 'stiff upper lip' for so long! Dick's wishes had been fulfilled.

So many people have told me it didn't feel like a funeral at all, that it was a 'lovely day' - save for the fact that it was Dick's funeral. I guess that is the best accolade of all – that is exactly how Dick would have wished everyone to feel – he wasn't a funereal person – he wanted laughing, jokes, stories – you can have all these yet still show respect. Long faces aren't a pre-requisite – after all to 'celebrate' someone's life, you must truly savour the spirit of the person – and Dick's smile was the order of the day.

For three consecutive Fridays we had emotional events to deal with, from the funeral, to the interment of Dick's ashes, and a Memorial mass at Peggy's church, Holyrood, in Watford.

It was a long hard three weeks coming on the back of those two weeks, two days since Dick's death.

Dick's ashes were interred at the top of the family grave, just outside the grave-set. The plot, in North Watford cemetery was purchased in 1959, when John junior died. His father joined him in 1986, now in 2007 they were both joined by Dick. I collected the ashes from the funeral directors myself that morning, allowing them briefly to sit once more in his favourite armchair. At the cemetery I walked from the office clutching the urn to my heart. I would never have imagined doing this, but I found it so comforting. My precious Dick had leaned on me these past few months, I wanted to carry him one last time and I badly needed that cuddle.

The grave is a simple one, so on the memorial tablet, together with his name and dates, the words "He touched the lives of everyone he met" were inscribed. It epitomises Dick's journey through life and was in keeping with the grave. I do not visit at specific times – I do so when I feel the need, but for the greater part I pay homage to Dick where it suits me best – at home and in the garden. I talk to him endlessly, and to the life-size photograph which now hangs on the wall overlooking the dining table - strategically placed behind the chair he occupied for our Saturday evening chats.

The Memorial mass was a lovely service, but I found it more upsetting – I guess I hadn't put my guard up, so emotions flowed more freely. It gave us all comfort, especially Peggy, of course.

I decided to return to work during the week following the Memorial mass. I made this decision after the funeral, knowing I had to set myself a goal – a target date for me to try to bring some normality back into my life – if that were at all possible. I had lost one and a half stone since December – half a stone quite literally 'vanished overnight' the day Dick died – it was time to put some of it back on.

So – what more about this man – Dick Pottinger? Well you've already got to know a great deal about him, but for me Dick's compassion for people and his gusto in life, made him so easy to love. He is truly the only man I've ever known to put everyone and everything else before himself. He would always be there to proffer a helping hand, would never pass by someone in need, and devoted much time in just giving of himself for the benefit of others. He liked people to be friends, hated animosity, and would always let you know if you were being uncharitable or bitchy. His kindness knew no bounds - he was generous with his money, but most importantly of spirit.

The personal loss to me is quite immeasurable – but notwithstanding I will always have the remembrance of the richness he bestowed upon my life to take with me.

His direct family, particularly Peggy and his sons are feeling the pain deeply and I know his friends and colleagues have a void they cannot fill. Dick is quite simply irreplaceable. I believe also that society has lost a true advocate and friend – an inspiration and participant of the highest calibre.

Of the multitude of sympathy messages I have received there are so many accolades attributed to Dick. Many adjectives and expressions were repeatedly used – *gentle; kind; warm; helpful; lovely man; wonderful man; an inspiration; true friend; very best of men; special; well respected; held in the highest esteem; much loved; admired; loyal; lucky to have known him; made a difference to the lives of others; compassionate; did so much for people* – the list is endless. He will be missed by so many, but never forgotten – and can be summarised in a quote from one card - 'The legend of the man lives on!'

CHAPTER 12

SOMEWHERE OVER THE RAINBOW

<u>We Will Always Be</u>

In the warmth of the sun I feel you
Igniting my spirit and soul,
In the scent of our roses I breathe you
Rebuilding me, making me whole.

In the sway of the breeze you touch me
Sending shivers the length of my spine,
In the song of the birds I hear you
Saying you'll always be mine.

In the still of the night you speak to me
Telling me all shall be calm,
In the light of the day lies your comfort
Keeping me safe from harm.

In my head every memory's a kiss -
A sweet image I cherish so dear;
In my heart lies our love forever
Knowing you'll always be here.

We may have been parted so early
When you were called to heaven above,
But I'm learning the secret of living
I've discovered the meaning of love.

We were blessed with each other my darling,
We lived life to the full every day
And laid foundations for our eternity
Nobody can take that away.

Know that I'm here with your spirit;
Know that I'm here with your soul;
Know that our love burns so brightly;
Know that you make me whole.

Know that you were so special -
The one saved by God for me;
Know that our love burns so brightly -
Know we will always be.

When the dust is settling on grief, and the numbness has totally worn off - you are given much time to reflect on what life has been, how it is now - and how you intend to move forward. Moving forward is what you must do - it is the only route to take.

Nothing can eradicate the memories of a life and loved-one - that is something no-one can take away from you. They are yours to keep and are a real blessing. I bought a hand-painted chest as a 'Memory Box' in which I have placed all manner of cards, artefacts, letters and objects that hold sections of my life with Dick. It is a comforting box and one I am happy to return to with frequency.

The commitment Dick and I had for each other was total - we never failed each other, not once. He made me the happiest woman on earth, and I too know that I gave him the happiness he so deserved - a happiness that had been missing for some time. It was an honour to be his wife, even if we failed to reach our seventh wedding anniversary on 7th July 2007. I, of course, miss everything about him - from the way he held his head to one side as he walked; to the looks he gave me.

He had a special look that said "I love you", and one more commonly used that plainly said "Shut up woman, you're talking too much".

Unlike me, Dick didn't voice his emotions freely, save for a Friday night when he invariably came home full of tales and anecdotes.

It was most often on Fridays, when he felt so happy and at peace with the world that he told me how much he loved me - usually making soppy statements to exaggerate the cause and hide his embarrassment at saying such things! More importantly, he never failed to actually show me he loved me - with his endless kindness and consideration.

People ask me if I am angry at what has happened. The truth is that I am not - what can I be angry at? I cannot be angry with Dick, nor the medical profession - okay so treatment delays did not help - but I am certain the outcome would have been the same. I can be angry at the cancer - but it won't change a thing. No amount of anger or bitterness would change my situation. Such negative emotions serve no purpose - unless self-destruction is your aim - although I can fully understand why others vent the depth of their loss in this way. However, I feel the recovery process and grieving is tough enough - without placing unnecessary burdens upon yourself.

You have to be patient but positive - the light will eventually emerge from the cloak of darkness. So, instead, I prefer to be thankful - grateful that I had the most wonderful time of my life with my lover, soul mate, companion and very best friend. I cannot complain.

For me it had seemed like I would never find my lifelong companion - and then along came Dick. Okay, so I am greedy, I wanted another eleven years with him, and another eleven after that but the quality of those eleven years we had together are worth my entire life. Sure I might feel cheated that our time together was comparatively brief - but I shouldn't. Some people never find something so good, so enduring or all-consuming - not even for five minutes.

Coping with bereavement will vary from person to person - quite naturally, since we are all unique, as are our relationships with others. The emotional trauma is the hardest to cope with, of course, but there is also a high volume of practicalities to go through before you can even begin the process of recovery.

Dick and I had, of course, taken care of the biggest issue - we had planned a funeral and set our house in order. Many people do not have the chance to make such preparations; therefore it is harder for them - especially at a time when, mentally, you are in some dark abyss and far from functioning well.

Having the computer makes letter-writing and communication easier and I am blessed with excellent organisational skills. Even beneath the veil of grief, I could at least perform these skills sufficiently in order to take care of the mountain of necessary correspondence. I wasn't prepared for the probate situation, especially as Dick and I painstakingly taken so much care to ensure our affairs were in order. I found it personally offensive and know Dick would have been horrified. Despite taking five months - this is at long last settled.

Having lived on my own for fourteen years prior to my life with Dick, I was also fortunate, in that being alone, running a house, dealing with finance, and fending for myself wasn't an issue. It is far harder for someone less independent, learning from scratch. I also feel, that being comparatively young (well forty-five going on forty-six to be precise) is an advantage as you tend to be more adaptable to change and generally more resilient. I am realistic and know that 'life must go on'.

Seeing couples does not trouble me, like I know it has other people in my situation - after all procreation would cease if it weren't for 'couples'. I do, however, find it tough when I see old couples out walking together - I concede to deep envy. I desperately wanted to grow old with Dick - to be in our dotage, yet still capable of holding hands and showing love for each other.

Having the incentive to cook again was not so easy. I had almost got out of the habit while Dick was in hospital as it was simpler to eat at hospital or nearby cafes - it made the work and hospital balance easier to achieve and gave some small respite to my days. For a time after losing Dick, with so many people running about with me and for me, I almost became a 'lady who lunches'. I had always envied such women and took advantage of this for a while - but it cannot continue indefinitely - and so I am now back into the habitual cooking and washing-up routine.

Another issue that couldn't be abandoned was the matter of Dick's accounts. As a bookkeeper I dealt with our respective business finances. While I am well-versed in dealing with end of quarter and end of year accounts - 'end of life' accounts was another matter entirely - it was so final, clinical and brutally difficult - there are no guidelines to help you deal with that one.

As I said earlier, I made certain changes, like sitting in Dick's chair, and spreading my clothes in the wardrobes, to minimise the huge void left by Dick's passing. These are only small things but they really made a significant difference to me.

From the offset I decided the traditions Dick and I had carried out together must be continued. I know Christmas will be poignant this year, but it will be a family occasion no less. I wanted to ensure the 'two mums' still had their mystery trip so I scheduled it early on, to give them dates for the calendar - an occasion to look forward to amidst the chaos life had thrown at us. It would have met whole-heartedly with Dick's approval. In early May I took them to Brockenhurst in the New Forest - we had a good time together, in spite of missing Dick dreadfully - he was such a lynch-pin to these trips. I set up a secret meeting with one of Peggy's nephews, wife and children, who live in the area. It rounded the trip on a high for Peggy.

In the first two weeks or so I took time to write personal family letters. I wrote to his sons, his mother and his first wife - I wanted them to know just how much Dick cared. I also wrote to baby Tristan - for when he is older, enclosing a copy of his grandad's photograph. I know Neil will tell him all about his father, but I wanted to tell him too.

As one who needs to keep busy I totally immersed myself in jobs and tasks to stop my brain from thinking too much. As we were planning to move house, we had intended to paint every room in the house this winter - a task we both hated the thought of, and which of course, was never done. I set about the job with a vengeance around the same time as I returned to work. My quest was to get it done before spring set in when I wanted to be out in the garden, where I knew I would find my salvation - my comfort - and Dick would be with me all the time. The incentive spurred me into a decorating frenzy. I could almost hear Dick's voice saying 'Don't forget to do the top of the doors' and 'You've missed a bit'. I confess I cursed him a few times as I worked around the house on this hated mission.

I cleared the debris from the top of the conservatory, with less agility than Dick, using his bargeboard to walk along. My sense of balance is none too clever and I was terrified of falling through the roof - but I survived unscathed - and at least the conservatory stopped leaking.

It was our garden that provided me with a true challenge, one I am sure Dick left for me on purpose. We have two handmade rustic pergolas and rustic fencing. These were all made by Dick and are fabulous features.

Dick had replaced the fencing and top pergola in recent years as the original rustic poles had rotted - the newer ones are more durable. He didn't however replace the one at the bottom of the garden - this being attached to the rustic fencing. I noticed it was perilously close to collapse, having rotted further over the winter and the weight of a mature climbing rose was leaning on it - making it even more precarious. If I didn't replace it, it would fall under the pressure, taking the fence with it. The gauntlet, therefore, was laid before me. Having acquired the poles I set to work one weekend.

Dismantling the old pergola was hard enough and propping up the fence, even more so, but somehow I managed. I then started building the new structure - relying on nothing but my recollection of how Dick had achieved it. He hadn't needed my help, so I knew it could be done single-handed - it was just a case of working it out and remembering.

Some six hours later, I had achieved the impossible. I was nothing short of ecstatic. I had been talking to Dick as I went, and am sure I had his divine guidance.

The poles were heavy and cumbersome to handle. Hammering for all I was worth I managed to wreck one finger and thumb as well as splitting another finger open - but what the heck - mission accomplished. It wasn't as perfect as Dick's and I made mistakes, but I will have learned from them - after all Dick's weren't so good to start with either. The sense of achievement was immense - now I knew that if I moved house I could replicate more of our garden than I had believed possible. The only negative force to arise was that the after the thrill of my accomplishment, I was left feeling low and aimless the following day. This is all just part of the roller-coaster ride that is 'grief'.

Moving house after losing your partner is something you have to consider very carefully. For mum, it was an almost immediate decision - and the best for her. With me it has been similar. I know I will move - hopefully back to my native roots - to Northchurch, where I feel safe and all things are familiar. I have always called it 'my other home' and Dick will know this is where I would go. The Cotswolds, as gorgeous though they may be, was our shared dream and not a move I wish to take alone. I have no intention of moving before the first year without Dick has passed - in any case I need 'our garden' this year to work its magic on me.

When I do move, I look forward to creating a new garden. I have learned so much from Dick and have his inspiration and creativity to work with. It will be planted and built for him as much as for me.

While you are battling with your own emotions, trying to make sense of all the madness inflicted upon you, you also have to deal with the reactions of other people. I recall when Martin was ill, a lady my mum had known all her life actually crossed the road, rather than face talking to her. It wounded mum deeply and I vowed I would never ever do that to others.

I would rather risk someone's tears, than to have them think I didn't care. Of course, this simply isn't the case in most instances – people genuinely care – they just don't know how to approach you. I have sympathy for those affected in this way – personally I find it is easier to be up front, and certainly since losing Dick, I'd much rather people be straightforward and blunt even, instead of treading on eggshells around me.

My neighbours could not have reacted in two more different ways. Our lovely friends, Bithi and Panu on one side, were so distraught at the loss of Dick, that they were unable to leave their house for two days. They have been wonderful neighbours - and now hold my spare door key in case I manage to accidentally lock myself out - which would be so easy to do - or need help, being here alone. My other neighbour by contrast, utterly confounded me one day when talking over the garden wall just three weeks after Dick's death. I thought he was having a ribald joke when he said, quite matter of fact "So are you over it now then?" I was speechless - especially when I realised he wasn't trying to be funny. As I said to him "I won't ever get over it - in time I guess I'll learn to live with it - but I haven't even started yet!" Insensitive? Maybe - or just totally ignorant - either way I was unimpressed!

Friends can also be an unknown quantity at times of trial and bereavement. Some become conspicuous by their absence - again, most often because they simply don't know what to say or do. Conversely, as with two of my friends, they re-emerge despite the fact that you have been out of touch for ages. I was fortunate to be reunited with two friends that I hadn't seen much of in recent years - Lesley and Theresa. Together with Val and Rosie they bought me a heart shaped pendant bearing an inscription of the final verse of that beautiful piece of prose 'Footprints'. This has been a favourite of mine ever since Martin's illness and was especially relevant now. It was a generous, kind touch. We have had some good 'girl's night's together' except for Rosie of course, being in America.

Rosie sent me the most beautiful e-mail, which had mum and I knee-deep in Kleenex tissues - she has a wonderful way with words, and expresses them freely in a way that only close friends do. When she came over to England in June, it was a very emotional first meeting. I had missed her so much - and she shared my pain and grief that Dick had been 'stolen' from me so soon.

Val and I have become very close - she has been a most wonderfully supportive friend and we meet up regularly for lunch or coffee and a chat. We used to work together, and although we socialised outside work we were very different people. Our relationship has certainly been taken to a different level of understanding these past few months - I am truly grateful for it and Dick would have been delighted.

Dick's friends and colleagues have been marvellous - not only with their tasks as pall-bearers and their kindness with the wake. The Outforce associates had a beautiful crystal claret jug engraved with the words 'The Richard Pottinger Memorial Trophy' - which will be played for on a special golf day each. The first was held on 12th June and I was honoured to present it to the winner. It is a fitting tribute to Dick, who would of course, much rather be playing golf, than being played for.

Our friend, Peter, re-framed the life-size photo for me as well as putting some of my favourite holiday photos into a multi-frame. I know it was difficult for him to do these things for me and I really appreciate his time and generosity.

Of course, burying yourself under tasks and challenges is all well and good - it helps keep the brain ticking and prevents too much dwelling on the events that have befallen you - but there is also the danger that you forget to grieve! I found I had so many invitations from people to call in, meet up or pop over. that I was fast running out of space for 'me'. Naturally, people have only the kindest intentions and want to help - they too feel helpless. There is, however, a danger of 'burn out' and I have found it vital to sit alone a while and be allowed to breathe.

As I work down a list of people to 'catch up with' I am being mindful not to try and do it all in a day. I am learning that I must sometimes say 'No', something neither Dick nor I were good at - but it is essential.

In the formative weeks after Dick's death I was in pieces first thing each morning, then it happened later in the day, but all the while I knew I hadn't really let go yet. We were half way through the year, yet I felt as if I had been caught in a time warp. I 'lost' the first three months of the year - I swear I woke up some time at the end of March, before the numbness finally wore off and I could start properly grieving. The shock had not fully dissipated. This volcano inside was fizzing and banging, with the odd rumble and explosion, but I knew, like a pressure cooker I had much steam to let off.

I had serious problems with appalling 'deathbed' images of Dick that infiltrated my sleep - so much so, that once awakened by them - no matter that it be three, four or five in the morning, I would have to get up. I couldn't return to sleep - and guess I was scared to try in case they returned. They were images transporting me back to Dick's dying moments - so vivid I could almost smell the ward. One image went beyond what I had seen to the point of decomposition, so you can imagine how traumatic the experience became.

I really didn't know how to tackle this dilemma. As much as I thought I was allowing my emotions freedom of expression and not trying to rush or force the grieving process - these 'images' were beyond my control. They were unbearably painful and having such a major impact on both my sleep and waking hours, I knew I couldn't let them continue unchecked without seeking help or advice.

Already aware of Grove House in St Albans, which offers a fantastic support network for both cancer sufferers and their families and carers, I phoned them. Their website - www.grove-house.org.uk gives comprehensive information as to the full range of services on offer. The Family Support Services kindly offered me counselling.

I have to say, I had, in the past, been somewhat scornful of the idea of counselling - seeing it as some form of 'cop out' for people not prepared to try and deal with issues in life themselves - not I surely - wasn't I made of stronger stuff after all? How wrong you can be!

I was to discover my preconceptions were completely false and I would advocate this service for anyone in need. I was, however, still sceptical as to whether it could be of benefit for my specific problem. I didn't feel that I had a problem with the 'grieving' itself - I am fairly pragmatic, level-headed and considered myself to be generally in control of this process, except for the 'images'.

On the first of my six sessions, I talked solidly for an hour. Talking to a stranger who has no emotional involvement is therapeutic and highly effective, especially one with such astounding listening skills. My counsellor allowed me to offload and except for picking up on some of the adjectives I used, didn't say too much.

Each session went deeper into my emotions and I found I was questioning myself throughout - my fears, worries and unanswered questions - the whole gamut. I could laugh, cry, rant or rave, it wouldn't matter - it was 'my time' to do or say anything I wished. There was no judgement, blame or criticism at any time which is particularly important when you are feeling so vulnerable. There was understanding, compassion, support and this voice of reason I knew I could tap into at any time.

A friend of mine then asked me if I'd written to Dick. Well I hadn't, as I was talking to him all the time inwardly - and out loud at home - where there was no-one to question my sanity. I asked my counsellor what he thought about this suggestion and he agreed it might be worth trying - after all I had written to everyone else - so why not to Dick? That particular session was my fourth, and by this time I had been taking notes in with me each week - based on questions or thoughts that had arisen during the intervening periods. Something seemed to click into place that day and I was a bit more emotional during my hour at Grove House. I drove home in tears - unearthing more from the depths of my inner anguish.

That afternoon I went for an Indian Head massage with a lady who does private treatments. I had, a few weeks earlier had one during a pamper day at Sopwell House, where I discovered I was way off the scale of one to ten in terms of stress-induced 'knottiness'. The private treatment was carried out from a more medical stance and was sensational. I was told I had 'rocks' not 'knots' trapped in all the stress areas she was to deal with. She worked from my back right through to my head. I could actually feel the tension moving from my back, up through my shoulders, up my neck and out of the top of my head. It was concurrent agony and ecstasy.

The following morning I felt hugely better. I had more energy, I had slept better and I had a freedom of movement in the head and neck that I almost didn't recognise. For the previous ten months, as the stress and tension increased, so my body had stored and held onto it. I had carried it around with me like excess baggage - battling against the tide and without there ever being a chance to dispose of it. My neck had felt like an immovable tree trunk. The lady also did some reiki with me, which unlocked yet more emotion. It was indeed a 'wet' day! Two weeks later I returned for another massage, which helped loosen up more knots - although the impact wasn't so striking due to the considerable improvement from that original visit.

I have since engaged Dick's osteopath who is making significant inroads toward restoring proper movement in my neck and back, which, in his words, were like cement.

My new rowing machine (yes Dick - I know - another piece of fitness equipment - but this one **is** being used I promise you) and my new found promise to go swimming a couple of times a week should also help to increase and maintain the flexibility. It is staggering that anxiety can cause such physical problems and is something everyone should be aware of.

On the Sunday morning - 20th May, I decided I would start my 'letter to Dick'. The following day I was taking mum on her special mother-daughter trip - we were off to Switzerland - a new discovery for us both. I was packed and ready to collect her in the afternoon, so I sat at the patio table with my laptop and let the words flow.

In writing to Dick, my face awash with tears, I asked him all the questions that had been bothering me - things I could never have a definitive answer to. No sooner had I committed them to paper than I got my answers. I was left with a deep feeling of inner peace and calm that has stayed with me ever since. I no longer needed to ask the questions. I considered this peacefulness to have emanated directly from Dick - after all I was the 'highly strung' one. In truth I probably simply really 'let go' of these burning questions. I had at last accepted what I could not change.

Mum and I had a fabulous trip to Switzerland. We crossed lake Lucerne on the boat and took the panoramic train down through the Alps, the Gotthard tunnel and on down to Lugano in the south. The weather was hot, scenery spectacular and we relaxed a great deal - we had both needed this break and made the most of it. The sheer beauty of the place tugged at my heartstrings - I had so wanted to bring Dick here - he would have adored it. He was, of course with me, for he never leaves me - I fervently prayed he could see the beauty too.

The day after arriving home, I was awakened early by the dustmen with their usual inconsiderate banging, crashing and talking at the tops of their voices. I forced myself back to sleep, only to be woken a short time later by a vision of Dick. He was walking down the driveway, his head leaning to the left as always, his hair like it had been on our wedding day, and with that 'smile' on his face. As soon as I realised it was him, so I woke - then tried desperately hard to go back to sleep - to see him again. It was so welcome to see my happy, healthy man again - and apart from a few very fleeting bad images I have not been disturbed by them again. Of course that's not to say they won't reoccur, but it is a significant step forward.

Our friend, Peter, again went that extra mile, when he gave me a short video clip with footage of the living, breathing Dick. All those mannerisms I know and love so well: the 'talking with his hands', the wise nod of his head, his smile, laugh, the irresistible twinkle in his eye and a face full of fun.

It is impossible to express the raw emotion that surfaced on seeing Dick alive again almost six months after his death. It was wonderful - yet painful - heaven and hell all at once - but I know for sure heaven will win! I am sure it will help me to keep the good image of Dick in place - it is a real treasure.

On my fifth counselling session, it was decided the sixth would be my last - and I worked towards it all week. It was another 'ending'. Having found a new friend I felt like I had lost him all too soon - I didn't realise how much I had come to rely on sharing my world and the support it had given me. I felt considerably wobbly for the weekend, but I knew now that there were others more deserving of this service. The job with me was in essence 'done'. It was up to me to move forward alone.

I have learned from the counselling experience that you should never knock anything until you have tried it - in combination with my own stoical approach it helped me immensely. You need never feel isolated as there are always people willing to help - you just need to open your mind and be receptive to it. A counsellor won't solve your problems single-handed - there must be willingness on your part to embrace the process and work with it.

I had promised Dick, long before he was ever ill, that I would never give up on my writing and it is with this in mind that I managed to resume this book, having started it some eighteen months earlier. Of course, from October 2006 when Dick's illness was diagnosed, until late June 2007 I had been in no frame of mind to write - Dick was most important, needed me 'full time' and the battle drained me of all else. After his demise, my emotions were so scrambled I had little chance of concentrating or finding words for this script.

I have always been one for making lists - this saved my bacon as my forgetfulness was dreadful. I would repeatedly ask friends the same questions and prayed they would understand that I had heard their answers - honest! It was just that my brain couldn't retain the information. It was at saturation point. The calendar became clogged with scribbled appointments for coffee, lunch or just 'popping' in to see someone or other. It was the only way I could keep a check on where I was meant to be and when, from one day to the next.

I know I still have a long way to go on the road to recovery. I am keeping positive, facing my fears and moving on. I am facing the year of 'firsts' with fortitude - some of which have already come and gone. I have also discovered that 'firsts' aren't confined to the major anniversaries.

The day following Dick's death long before dawn was breaking I arose from fitful dozing, alone for the first time to this new life without Dick; next there was the first of many times I have caught myself saying 'I must tell Dick about that'. I have to catch myself when shopping - not to put his favourite doughnuts in the trolley, and to walk past clothes I know would look fabulous on him.

Then there are parties or functions – some of which I have encountered thus far, with another advancing on me swiftly. Turning up alone is daunting and I am learning that it is easier to arrive early and have crowds gradually come in behind me, than to walk in late after the crowds have formed. So there are ways of coping – you just have to find a mechanism that works for you.

I am finding it impossible to gauge what my reactions to each big 'first' will be. On Dick's birthday – 31st March – I awoke to the thought that I don't love Dick any more or less today than I did yesterday, or will tomorrow – so why should the day be any different – except for the poignancy of the date? This made perfect sense until I visited the cemetery and was perturbed to find myself in shreds and utterly inconsolable.

Over and again in my head I asked "Where would we be right now - where would I have taken him this year?"

Last year on this date we had been in Rome - walking our legs off between the tourist traps and clutching each others hands as we raced across roads avoiding the maniacs on Vespa scooters; the year before that we had pounded the streets of London and ridden on the London Eye for the first time; and the year before that it had been Barcelona with its wonderful Gothic quarter and sitting in Las Ramblas drinking coffee. My confidence plunged into the depths of despair despite my waking revelations.

On 7th July, I went on a pilgrimage to Castle Combe accompanied by my dear friend Rosie, while she was over from the United States. I awoke in reflective mood, unable to visualise how the day would unfold – nor my response to it. We set off in good time and stopped off at Burford, Oxfordshire en route. Rosie has ancestral connections to this beautiful village, and I of course had special memories of a weekend there with Dick. As we drove down into the High Street my spirits soared – all the wonders of our trip flooded back and I couldn't help smiling, laughing and remembering such a good time spent there. I instinctively knew the day was to be a good one.

As we arrived at Castle Combe so my heart and stomach raced with the million butterflies that had invaded my body on our wedding day. The village, as sublime as ever, touched me as only Castle Combe can. Despite a sign saying the Manor House was closed due to an event, thankfully we found the way was only barred for vehicles – we walked through the grounds and retraced the steps of my wedding.

A beautiful bride and her party were on the lawns in the hands of their photographer. Lucky lady – she too will have this treasure to take with her for life. Rosie and I walked into the Manor House then up through the beautiful Italian gardens. It was heaven – a wonderful moment. I felt the rush of love coursing through my veins and know now this place will evoke nothing but the happiest of times for me.

As Rosie and I meandered our way home through bucolic England, I felt inspired and confident that I would be able to revisit places shared with Dick with a lighter heart. Yes of course, there was a tinge of pain, but those treasured moments became the focal point - the strongest force and that is how I wish it to stay. Yet for all that I began questioning my sanity and felt guilty - shouldn't I be upset? Or is it just that others might expect me to be so? Expectations again - and not always mine. Peer pressure does play a part in grieving. People tend to form opinions of how you should behave or feel and when you should feel it. Mum said she almost felt guilty to catch herself laughing for the first time after dad had passed away - I can totally empathise with her. We all expect too much of each other at times which does nothing but add to the pressures that we place on ourselves to conform to the 'norm' whatever that is. I have considered this since returning from Castle Combe and, of course, I know it is quite ridiculous. There are no rules to this process. It is okay to feel how you do, whatever that may be. All things will become rationalised in the end.

The major 'firsts' for me will culminate in the anniversary of Dick's death 10th January 2008. I am not afraid to face such painful episodes and in some strange way almost welcome them as they make me stronger with their passing. The emotional outcome is not so important - but being prepared to embrace them most definitely is. Anniversaries of any kind evoke memories - be they good or bad. Sometimes you just have to look a bit harder to find the 'good' memory within the bad. As yet I cannot think of anything good about 10th January 2007, save for the display of deep love from close family and friends - that then is the key to my survival.

It is vital to have a focus - a purpose to your life - and I will strive to be the best I can in all I do. I am determined, if nothing else to make Dick proud of me - to know that I am fulfilling both our philosophies of life and death. We will always 'be' - Dick and I - our relationship was unique to us. It has been the most uplifting, magical and complete phase of my life - one in which I have grown so much as a person, thanks to the Dick's love. As I continue my earthly journey and enter the next phase, I know Dick will want me to 'live life' to the full. I can smile, laugh, love and be happy - he would expect nothing less.

When I took a trip out to stay with Rosie on her alpaca farm in the late summer I was deeply moved by the surprise that she and Ric had waiting for me. A seat going round a shady tree overlooking the female alpacas' pasture had a plaque on it bearing the words 'Dick's Spot - Our Caring Friend'. What a lovely gesture and so fitting. I spent my first cup of tea each day in quiet reflection on this seat as I gazed at the beautiful alpacas. I felt their calming influence and shared my thoughts with Dick in this place. I could still picture him running excitedly from the barn the last time we stayed. He had stumbled across a tarantula running across the floor and couldn't wait to show me (I wasn't so keen for the experience myself!). I also saw him helping Ric with new fencing - this was a good place to come. The peaceful alpacas, my dear friends and 'Dick's Spot' all assisted the recovery process. Yes I had tears, but I also had solace.

This year's Friday Club French golf trip was again at Le Touquet, France where they had a special dinner, courtesy of Dick. As Dick's best friend, I gave Paddy Dick's golf clubs - he tells me he played better than ever with them. The guys stayed at the Westminster Hotel - and were delighted when they were allowed to hang a photograph of Dick next to those of celebrities who had stayed there previously. Of course Dick was a 'star' to me and all of his friends, so he is well placed. It was another lovely touch for which I am grateful. Dick's life continues to touch others - his memory will live on. He would also have been tickled pink by Paddy who provided the fun this year. He got to France only to find he had left his clothes behind - how Dick would have laughed!

I know that the very things that break my heart now will sustain me - I already feel that Dick is passing some of his strength back to me and can feel his healing touch on my heart. I know he will always provide me with the most special inspiration. I will see him in every twinkling star, every kiss of the sun, brush of the breeze and bite of frost. He is birdsong and silence - but most of all he is in my heart, mind and soul. I am trying to take my memories of him from sadness and to let the joy of the man shine through - that way his spirit will last forever.

I believe that in writing my letter to Dick on 20th May I took a gigantic step along the path to recovery. It is naturally very personal but if by sharing it, it can help others to understand some of the thought processes that hurtle through the brain at such times then I am happy to do so. Recognition of the questions and issues involved goes part-way to solving them.

20th May 2007
My darling Dick,

How do I begin to tell you all that I feel right now? For once words seem to elude me, but I feel I must try to speak to you if only to clear my head.

I don't need to tell you how much you mean to me. You really were the special, irreplaceable one 'true love' that was destined to be mine. How grateful I am for all that we shared and for the eternal memories you have given me, they are mine until I am once more with you.

While your body is no longer a physical presence in my life, your love and spirit will never leave me – our souls will always be entwined. I will keep you alive in my heart and thoughts.

Did we know – deep down, that this cancer was going to tear us apart? Yes – I think so. From the moment you started being ill last summer, I knew we were in trouble. I prayed that it was something like the diverticulitis again – I had been so convinced you had bowel cancer then and so wrong, that this time I tried to control my anxiety.

As things got progressively worse I became so scared. I'm sure you were too, but together we could be strong – keep positive and know that we would deal with it all together. When the cancer became a diagnosis, my heart almost shattered on the spot. I knew that your constitution was not like Martin's – that your body and strength were going to have to overcome huge obstacles. Food has never been important to you - you never relished a meal or displayed a good appetite – except for those lovely breakfasts you craved. I knew that unless we could keep your food intake up things would prove tough – really tough. The oesophageal cancer was a pig – it never gave you the chance to build up your strength. Every step forward, when we finally got treatment under way, meant a further three steps back.

I know at times we got cross with each other – you, out of frustration, and me out of fear. It didn't matter – we knew we were there for each other no matter what.

I am so glad we took the time to plan your funeral, although I never for one moment imagined we would have to instigate it so very soon. I will never forget that day, not ever. It's strange, but all the music we chose we had no idea to use in what order or way. The moment it was needed, I knew instinctively what went where.

I still look at the picture of you with darling Tristan – and realise how pale and drawn you were. The look that passed between us went unspoken didn't it? You knew what I was thinking and I knew you knew – that this might be the last picture of you with your grandson. I can't now be sure if it was – but believe so by your pallor.

He's a beautiful little boy, now crawling and I know you will be watching over him with love. He will be brought up to know what a special grandad he had. It just breaks my heart that he won't get to share with you that special relationship – your love and guidance would have been such an inspiration to him. I will try to make sure that I can pass on your wisdom to him.

I think back to Christmas – I am so glad you got to sit in your armchair once more, and had I known what was going to happen, I would have brought you back home again on Christmas Day. I think you understand why we couldn't do this – you were so unwell at home – and without fluids and drip feeds you would have moved on even quicker. Nevertheless I do regret not having you here on that day. I'm so glad you got to see Tristan – although I felt your frustration at not being able to reach or hold him again.

Somewhere Over the Rainbow

If I had known that chemotherapy was going to make no difference I would have told them not to bother with that either. I can still feel your indignity when diarrhoea hit you at Mount Vernon – my sweet, sensitive man - I know how terrible that was for you.

At Watford you were counting the days to the operation. Like you, I thought this would only help us turn a corner – although I was petrified that the operation itself might kill you. I know it didn't instantly, but your body was so weak – there was nothing left to fight with.

I'm glad you saw the boys and Pat and Mike. I'm sad that David never got to see you and I know it now tortures him with regret. I'm so sorry you never got to read that final card from your mum.

I was right in the card I sent you and read to you after the operation – love is not the person you see yourself with – it is the person you cannot see yourself without. That is now my own personal battle.

Val and I cried at the Three Hammers with relief that you were back from the operation safely – I had been so scared of losing you. You looked so ill after the operation – it wasn't you that came back was it? You looked worse than after the diverticulitis operation. I didn't stay too long that day as you needed to recover gently. I spoke to you and I know you knew I was there.

The following day I was shocked as you were still on the oxygen and looked terrible. Again it tore me in two to see you suffering so much. You woke up when you needed to – like to tell me Dr Livingstone said the operation was successful and had I spoken to him – my darling I had only just arrived.

I only got to see the junior doctor in the end and he couldn't tell me much – only that the blockage in your small intestine appeared to be another tumour – he said that I needed to speak to one of the people present at the operation. That is the truth my love – and when you looked at me for an answer I knew I could only reiterate what Dr Livingstone had told you.

They didn't just stitch you back up love – they did do the op, but it wasn't what they wanted. I couldn't put more fears into your head until I knew the facts properly – please forgive me darling. I am sure you already knew there was more to tell – I'm not a good liar – but you were so unwell it would have been wrong to say more. What I didn't know was that they had also found stomach cancer – that is why the stent had no effect – together with the intestinal tumour.

It was right the way through darling – how could we have known things would move so fast. You would have had awful pain to come and still I don't feel you would have been able to beat this – it was too much. I am only glad you were spared this pain – for neither of us would have coped with it – in different ways.

That day you waved me away with your hand. Did you know or feel this was the time – were you sending me away to spare me – or were you just needing peace and solace. When I came back for the card to take home with me I caught a tear at the corner of your eye. Was it the oxygen causing your eye to water – or was it a tear? If it was a tear I pray your weren't stopping me from comforting you. It was the last time I could have spoken to you and have known you could hear me.

That night I went to visit Paddy & Cheryl. I told them the truth and my fears. I knew Paddy had an onerous task ahead of him and felt it might be far sooner than we had expected. They tried to reassure me – we were speculating. I spent three hours at their house and we covered most scenarios – except the one that the following day brought to us.

That next morning I was weirdly focused at work, until I took the call from the hospital. I knew then it was to be the worst of days – the call was carbon copy of the one mum took when dad had died. I thought I had already lost you – and I guess technically I had. I drove sensibly – somehow to the hospital but it took me forty minutes to get there. I paid for a parking ticket, abandoned the car in torrential rain and ran to the ward. I was whisked into the side room and told basically that you were dying. You had stopped responding.

Dr Livingstone's team were there to answer questions I might have, but I could only think then of being with you, my precious husband. I wasn't prepared for how you would look, your eyes had rolled back and corneas were already sticky. The oxygen was all that kept you alive. The machines had all gone and a nurse sat holding your hand. Darling as I sat on your bed talking to you – could you hear me – please God I hope you knew I was with you and would never leave you. Did you feel that final kiss I gave you? Your hands at least were warm, but your mouth so cold – again maybe it was the oxygen causing that? It was so hard knowing the rest of the ward could hear me talking to you. It was torture watching and waiting until the last breath left your body. It was oh so painful, I loved you more than I could ever love myself or another and I miss you so desperately.

I wanted to thank you, my love, for all that you have been and always will be to me. I know I made you happy, but still needed reassurance that you were truly happy with me. I hoped I had been to you some of what you are to me. I tried to bring you laughter, fun and joy – and we had all that in abundance didn't we?

The nurse helped me to take your wedding ring off – it went straight from your hand to mine darling, and apart from two days being made to fit my wedding finger it has not and never will be off my hand. It symbolises our love – two wedding rings separated only by an eternity band – no, I didn't need an engagement ring – you were right. If I'd had one I would not be able to wear our two bands together, so I am glad.

My 'Bunny' – I just pray that when you stopped responding that you had entered a peaceful sleep – one in which you could hear me one last time telling you how much I loved you. I pray you did not suffer – you had done enough of that over the previous few months.

I went into shock when you had breathed your last. It was simply terrible having to pack your belongings with your body lying on the bed – I felt like I was invading your space. I know that your spirit and soul had already flown – to a place where nothing can hurt you ever again. I felt like a huge part of me had died with you and the rest of me had been left behind in hell. That of course isn't true – while I am still here I carry you with me everywhere – so that can never be hell. I just cry out to have you here with me still – never to be apart.

I called Paddy and he was as inconsolable as I was – we sobbed together uncontrollably, until he needed to go out for air. He came to see you – incidentally I suspect you know all that I am telling you – I am sure you were looking down on us in sympathy and with the tenderness only you possessed. I phoned David and Michael – that was so hard.

Michael came back to be with your mum – your poor, darling mum – who's first thoughts were for me and not herself. Paddy phoned the boys. I phoned Martin so he could go to my mum. I didn't want her coming to the hospital but needed her with me at home later. She has been so wonderful as always. She was grief-stricken too – she adored you. Cheryl and Mary arrived at the hospital – they were fantastic.

When we left the hospital to go home I was in total shock, the brandy didn't touch the sides – the same brandy that usually gives me a thumping head turned into my saviour – as it did at your funeral.

You were with us all at home – although your mum had gone home – later that evening we sat there – our wedding party again! We chose well our friends my love – there for the very happiest and saddest of times.

You know – what I feel so much – apart from my own personal loss, which is immeasurable – I feel society and so many people have lost so much by your premature passing. You gave so much of yourself – always to others first, always putting yourself last. I always felt you had so much more to do and to give, such joy to share and bring to others.

I know that you made life richer for oh so many people: your loved ones and friends of course, but also work colleagues and victims alike – even at times 'defendants' as you bought them a lunch.

If by your passing, it has made people aware of what they have lost that is no bad thing – maybe they can take the lessons you spread and use them and learn from them to everyone's benefit.

Your funeral had some four-hundred people there – were you watching love? It was overwhelming. Paddy's address was excellent, as was Dave Perry's. Steven did you so proud – a wonderful tribute on behalf of him and Neil – and Tristan slept peacefully throughout – God love him. We chose the music well. I was taken aback when walking in behind you to 'Everything I Do' – our joining together and parting song. 'Bring You Home' by Ronan Keating was an inspired decision. That track brings me so much comfort and the words are so supportive to everything I know you would feel and say to me – as well as others. You are always there, I am never alone, but I also have to carry on living – be all that I can be. I will pick up the threads of my writing again – and in truth my letter to you is just the first step.

You have now rewritten my autobiography with a final chapter that will be so hard to write – in hindsight, maybe it shouldn't be the last chapter – maybe the final chapter should encompass living and moving forward – I don't know yet – it will be settled when I write it no doubt.

When Friends by The Osmonds played, Nikki tells me the sun came out from behind the clouds and illuminated the crematorium – spooky eh? No – just you, underlining the message within the song. If people can be friends with each other then your message is not in vain.

I'm sorry but I did allow a police guard of honour in the end – I know you conceded only to the drape, but the pride of the guard of honour was a touch I felt your sons and mother deserved. You so richly deserved the honour for all that you gave. It was an added mark of respect. I didn't need it for myself as I already knew the respect with which you were held – by me more than anyone, but I am glad I did it – your humility would have prevented what was so justly yours.

The wake was supplied by the Friday Club – a typical 'police bash' that thankfully for me I was fully comfortable with. Brandy kept me going all afternoon and evening – the adrenaline must have been racing through me. I said a few words on your behalf darling – without slurring my words, nor falling off my heels – see the brandy worked. I so wanted you to be proud of me – I think I did okay all in all that day. I wore my lovely black cocktail dress with long black jacket, my wedding jewellery and heels. I wanted to wear something you loved and it matched perfectly.

I have the life-size photo of you – they enlarged the one from the cruise – ironic isn't it – you didn't want me to buy that picture – but I'm so glad I did – I was obviously meant to. It gives me such comfort and I talk to you through it frequently – you are still at the head of the dining table. I stared at your picture through the entire funeral service, talking to you silently. I kissed it when Dave handed it to me.

The original picture is so animated – I see your eyes twinkle and smile – as if you're about to burst into your glorious laugh that touched everyone. My favourite wedding picture is also on the bedside cabinet and I have two miniatures in my purse.

You are also on the new mobile phone so I see your face at the flick of the screen. So you see – physically I'm trying to keep the happy and healthy you with me to match the soul and spirit, which can never leave me.

The bad luck continued for a while that dreadful week – can you believe 'Locate' had not got our original wills! So Phil is sorting out probate for us. I know you would be furious – I certainly was, as we took so much care to look out for each other didn't we – up to planning the funeral?

The police managed to pay your full pension in February, and my bank cancelled my direct debits and cash card! Still that was just one or two blips that are now sorted. The heating packed up when snow was forecast and the toaster overheated. The washing machine and shower started leaking but corrected themselves – or did you help out there?

Can you believe that you had two winning premium bonds the day before you died – you had only been saying you'd had none for a while. Not only that you've had more since! You must be making the draw yourself love.

I have been having problems with the deathbed images left with me that morning 10th January. They have woken me up on several occasions and I am seeing a counsellor to try to help with this. June Lynch tells me it could be my way of saying 'I'm not ready to let go yet' – I don't know.

The intelligent, rational me knows you are gone, but my emotional side and heart still cannot believe it. I think that is the problem and I know time will help but it can be so hard. I don't know if the images will ever go completely, as they can never be turned to a happy memory and are very traumatic. It was such a painful moment – maybe that is why they haunt me so – my mind cannot deal with that level of pain. Or is it just I have unanswered questions – were you at peace? Could you hear me? I only wish I knew. I pray that you could visit me one night instead as a friendly ghost sitting on my bed talking to me, telling me you're at peace and fine and that I will be fine too.

I miss that Friday Club night when you would come home and in your own touching, lovable way call me your 'sweetie' and tell me how much I mean to you and that you love me. I miss your little tales and funny golf stories. I miss the look that says 'I love you' and the look that says 'Shut up woman, you're talking too much'.

I miss the plans we made together, for the garden, moving house and our marvellous travel adventures and weekend breaks. But what I miss in that has become a special memory. I have created a memory box now with so much in it. I miss moaning about your accounts, 'tutting' at never getting a chance to talk as you were always on the phone – and I will never moan again at having to cut the grass.

I wrote letters to your mum, Angela, the boys and Tristan as I wanted them to know how much you cared. I also wrote to Auntie Kitty as she wrote to me after you had died, unknowingly. She tells me that my love for you shines through from the written word – well I was always good with words wasn't I?

I still hear all the charity news – they are learning more about you since you passed away and I am a sounding-block – being the closest to you – as they think I might have your same perspective on things.

I am trying hard to be more like you. I try to be as kind and benevolent as you although I'm sure I fail at times. I am trying to see things through your eyes and the shining example you have set me. I will continue to try and live my life better – be more like you in every way. I have washed away the resentment I felt at the way you have been spoken to and treated by some people, save one and I am glad about this.

The garden is my salvation at the moment. I had to replace the red azalea which was past its best. Then, as you will know – there was the pergola you hadn't replaced! I swear you left it for me on purpose!! Well I had to use some skill to keep the bottom fence from collapsing so I could batten the new pergola to it. I made mistakes and it wasn't anywhere near as good as your last one – but I think you would have been impressed. I had obviously watched you more closely than I realised and managed to achieve it. I was so thrilled

– now when I move house I can build us another garden and replicate many features we had here. I have been taking cuttings and written a list of plants that I want – they will be all our favourites. I picked your first 'Felicia' to flower this year, to have it indoors. 'Compassion' is starting to flower, 'Seagull' is just starting to open – the garden is so full of your skills and love. I know wherever I go I will feel your touch in the garden, whatever I plant, create or do, will be with you in mind – listening to your heart and learning from your creativity. You have given me so much more than 'love' – you have taught me so much about myself, people and life – I will always be in your debt

I now have a newer Micra – a red one this time – called 'Felicia' after your favourite rose – it was tough trading the Almera in – so many times I have expected to hear it pull up, over that wobbly slab.

So many times I have sat at the patio table as if waiting for you to return from work. Too many glasses of red wine taken alone – I am watching and mindful of that darling – it has just helped at times. The green table under the conifers is hard to sit at – our table for two. I now sit in your chair, rather than looking at it empty – I couldn't bear that. I feel closer to you that way as well.

You of course, know that I will move back to Northchurch. The pipe dream of the Cotswolds was a shared one – and not for me to take on alone. I have stored the document and plans in the memory box as we had such fun didn't we – ticking boxes and dreaming. Still – what is life if not for having a few unassailable or unrealised dreams – if there is nothing to aim for, there is no joy. I won't go this year as I need to be in our garden – it is a huge part of my healing. I just hope I get the timing right as there isn't much on the market right now. The bungalow was valued at a price far higher than we could have expected – you wouldn't have believed it love. It makes me more hopeful of being able to find something affordable and suitable later.

I look at our holiday pictures, Peter kindly framed some for me – what fantastic times we had, what journeys. We never had a bad trip did we? Even the weekend breaks were perfect – we made the best of everything- rain or shine. We were lucky – it was mostly 'shine' wasn't it? And that is how I must continue – to make the best of things.

Peter has been fabulous – putting in the odd phone call to see how I'm faring. Just bad luck the last two times he's called I have been on a down day. Well hopefully next time I will be sprightlier.

I took the 'two mums' away to the New Forest for their mystery trip. It was tough without you – there was a big hole where you should have been. I'm sure we all felt it – not just me, but we packed lots in – went back to our adored Exbury gardens – and took the buggy this time to help your mum out. We even got to see Colin and Katie at Lymington before coming home, which pleased Peggy enormously. The hotel was a bit tired and internet description deceptive, but still we had a good time.

Peggy is doing very well. Naturally, like me she is heartbroken. She held a memorial mass for you, as you would know she would do. I found it hard and emotional, but her friends did her proud and are so supportive of her. I have taken her shopping and to the library and decorated her lobby as a surprise for her while she went off to Devon. I am trying to help her as much as possible – I will always be there for her love – but you are an impossible act to follow – no-one, not even David and Michael can replace you for her – there was always only one Richard. You had a relationship with her akin to that of a mother and daughter - now I know why you were supposed to be a daughter 'Mary'! She loved you so much and takes with her the fact you gave her such confidence and were her counsellor and friend as well as such a cherished son.

Your ashes are with your dad and brother John now. We have put a memorial tablet down – kept simple like the grave site – but I added 'He touched the lives of everyone he met' as it sums up you and what you mean to so many people. I don't go the grave frequently as I know you wouldn't want me to stand there weeping – I am better in tune with you at home, in the garden and with my deepest thoughts.

I have a dilemma as to where I should go when I move on. My ashes could be put with yours, although I don't know what the rest of the family would feel about that. Personally I am happy to be scattered on Northchurch Common with the deer! Trouble is you never saw the deer, so would you be able to find me!? I think so – for we will be together always. My spirit will know just where to find you when the time comes.

Linda Pottinger

I am taking mum away tomorrow – to Switzerland. I know you grouched when I suggested that as my next trip for her – 'I haven't been there' you said. Well my love, tomorrow you will be there, with me, looking at the wonderful scenery. Mum has been such a darling to me – you died six days before dad's 10th anniversary - can you believe that? I hope you've got to say hello to him for me and to let him know how much I miss and love him too. I was so glad he got to meet you – he already thought the world of you.

Steve has got engaged to Ciony – well there's a thing – at least he didn't just get married. I will no doubt hear all about it when he gets back. I know you'd be pleased – if not a little anxious about it. I'm sure it will all work out in the end and he's a big boy now. I think he and Neil have both matured in losing you – their beloved dad.

They have been very supportive to me. They are keeping an eye on me, like I'm sure you asked Steve to that day at Hemel hospital - when he got upset. Both your sons are decent, kind human beings and have been wonderful – thank you. They treated me, mum and Peggy to dinner one Sunday and bought me a card and flowers on Mothers day. You would have been so pleased, not to mention proud. Well take pride now darling. I met, and liked Angela too.

I must also thank you for that other 'task' left for me - the decorating of the bungalow! After the funeral and just as I was returning to work I decided to make a start on that winter job we were sadly unable to do. All those new doors got cursed at. I chatted to you as I worked – could hear you saying 'don't forget the tops of the doors' and 'you've missed a bit'.

I was like a woman possessed and did it all. It is hard to accomplish chores you hate doing – but maybe it was good therapy at the time – anyway I wanted it done so I could enjoy the garden. We had a very dry, warm and sunny April – you wouldn't believe that I cut the grass first in March either – spooky. It's made up for it with the first two weeks in May being very wet – like the year we last had a dry April. I didn't forget your clematis – remembered to prune them for you. Everything is earlier this year.

As I write today I can hear the chirruping of baby blue tits (or Great tits) in your nesting box on the silver birch. At least Humphrey can't scare them away. It's funny but you are a flower and garden to me, not so much a bird – but if it has to be a bird you may be a blue tit – so cute, delicate and joyful. Now you can befriend the blackbird and robin synonymous of dad and Grandpy.

My other friends have been brilliant as well as Paddy, Cheryl and Mary, of course. I've spent lots of time with Cheryl. Paddy is finding it hard – he didn't like the Friday Club without you, but is going fairly regularly again now. They were thinking of not doing the golf trip – but I was mortified and told Paddy you would really not be happy about that. You wanted them to have fun and they at least have the funds to do just that with - they plan to have a 'slap-up' meal in your honour - and have now booked it so I'm pleased. Like us all it has taken them time to readjust to life without 'Dick' – I feel like I haven't even started myself.

Rosie comes over in June and when I get to see her I am sure it will be emotional for us both. Val has been a rock, and is having a tough time herself. We have become extremely close and it is good to have built bridges with her - I am very grateful for that. I've also got to see Lesley and Theresa again – it's nice to think my friends are still there despite the contact we missed out on for a while – and all because of you sweet darling.

On a Hedgehogs golf day someone moaned about the greens too much and Dick McGregor said 'Dick Pott would love to be playing on these greens'. It stopped the moaning quickly. So you see my darling – you still have huge impact on others. Gary says it was lonely that first golf day without you.

I've not heard much from some of your other friends but I know they don't know what to say to me, which is understandable. You had a way of affecting everyone on a deep and personal level – it is not just I who feels so lost without you.

Well love, for today this is as much as I can write. My head is somewhat clearer than when I started writing to you today. I am emotionally adrift and dare I say almost unhinged at times – I am fine one minute, then the sledgehammer crashes down on me taking my legs away. I feel despair at times, but all the while I know the love of you will rebuild my hope and future. My broken heart won't mend overnight, if ever – I will have to learn to live with it although I will never get over losing you – not really.

You were given to me for eleven glorious years. We licked each others wounds, and really gave life a good bash didn't we? We had a ball you and I – more ups than downs and barely a cross word.

You always managed to sort my head out in the end, even if you had to get tough with me – but I thank you for that – you have given me a better balanced life and I feel better equipped to cope with all life throws at me – although for now that won't be so apparent.

Look down on me my love and know for always I will keep you in my heart. God bless you.

Your ever loving plump-p xxxxxxxxx

I would like to finish this book by sharing a verse I was given very recently - to me it epitomises the way forward. I apologise to the author as it was unsigned. I think it is quite beautiful. As I read it I realised I am on the way to making the right choices - the ones I see as the *only* choices! Yes, there are dark days, but out of the gloom a chink of light beckons me ever forward.

You can shed tears that he is gone, or you
can smile because he has lived.
You can close your eyes and pray that he'll come back,
or you can open your eyes and see all he's left.
Your heart can be empty because you can't see him,
or you can be full of the love you shared.
You can turn your back on tomorrow and live yesterday,
or you can be happy for tomorrow because of yesterday.
You can remember him only that he is gone, or you
can cherish his memory and let it live on.
You can cry and close your mind, be empty and turn your back - or
you can do what he'd want: smile, open your eyes, love and go on.

END

Somewhere Over the Rainbow

Tristan    Dick & Tristan - Oct 06    My pergola!

Memorial tablet    On the wall at Westminster Hotel, Le Touquet

Dick's Spot at Rosie & Ric's    My beloved Dick

Printed in the United Kingdom
by Lightning Source UK Ltd.
125608UK00001B/151-297/A